Endorsements

"Your story is so compelling — quite the faith-builder, as you share the many ways God is so personally involved in the details of your life! These are beautiful stories of your own humanity and suffering, beyond your physical suffering, in relationship to your father. So many of us have "daddy issues" that affect us from childhood all the way into our adult years. I think many will be able to relate. I know I did."

LISA WHELCHEL, ACTRESS, AUTHOR, & LIFE COACH

"For anyone who has ever questioned the creativity and beauty of God's plan, *When I Wished upon a Star* is the perfect read. This story truly touches the soul."

JONATHAN HORTON, OLYMPIC GYMNAST &
AMERICAN NINJA WARRIOR

"The connection between Phillips and the sitcom star is legitimately intriguing, and readers...might see the hand of God at work in this story. An earnest, inspiring memoir for Christian readers and fans of *Growing Pains*."

KIRKUS REVIEWS

WHEN I
WISHED
UPON A STAR
From Broken Homes to Mended Hearts

WHEN I
WISHED
UPON A STAR

From Broken Homes to Mended Hearts

Brandon Lane Phillips, MD
&
Jeremy Miller

THOMAS NELSON

Since 1798

thomasnelson.com

When I Wished upon a Star
From Broken Homes to Mended Hearts

Published in Nashville, Tennessee, by Thomas Nelson. Thomas Nelson is a registered trademark of HarperCollins Christian Publishing, Inc.

Thomas Nelson titles may be purchased in bulk for educational, business, fund-raising, or sales promotional use. For information, please e-mail SpecialMarkets@ThomasNelson.com.

This book reflects the authors' present recollections of experiences. The names and identifying details of some individuals have been changed to protect their privacy. Some events have been compressed, and some dialogue has been re-created.

The authors are represented by Ambassador Literary Agency, Nashville, Tennessee.

Library of Congress Cataloging-in-Publication Data

Pre-Launch ISBN 978-1-595558428

Library of Congress Control Number: 2018948920

ISBN 978-1-595558411 (Paperback)
ISBN 978-1-595558565 (Hardbound)
ISBN 978-1-400332878 (Casebound)
ISBN 978-1-595558114 (eBook)

DEDICATION

For our mothers,
Carolyn Wagoner Phillips
and
Sonja "Sonny" Southworth

Contents

INTRODUCTION

Back when TV was on only three channels—ABC, NBC, and CBS—I was playing Mike Seaver on the set of *Growing Pains*. The cast and I were meeting kids with cancer and other serious illnesses week after week through several wish-granting organizations. One day a young boy with a heart defect visited our set—not to see me particularly, but to visit my fellow cast-mate, actor Jeremy Miller, who played my younger brother Ben Seaver on the show. Little did I know that his wish to visit the set of his favorite sitcom would later result in him becoming my trusted friend, middle-of-the-night family doctor-on-call, and an inspiring man of faith whose life story continues to amaze me. In *When I Wished upon a Star*, Brandon Lane Phillips and Jeremy Miller bring together many seemingly random circum-stances to form a beautiful tapestry of love, friendship, hope, and healing.

My dear friend Jeremy Miller could have easily become just another Hollywood statistic were it not for the divine interven-tion of a God who cares, honors wishes, and, yes, answers prayers. I can't wait for you to read how Brandon and Jeremy's lives inter-twined and unfolded to bring them to where they are today!

Neither I nor Jeremy knew it at the time, but for some reason, Mike Seaver and his little brother Ben were supposed to be lifelong friends with a kid from Louisiana with a heart condition. Years after *Growing Pains* had ended, I reconnected with Brandon while I was on a movie set in Canada. To be honest, I didn't know what to expect. After all, Brandon's "wish" to visit the *Growing Pains* set was because of his ailing heart, and I wasn't sure he would even be alive after all of these years. I certainly had no idea of how his life had taken such an amazing turn and become a dynamic example of God's love, power, and even...sense of humor!

Brandon has since become our family's 2:00 a.m. on-call doctor, calming my dad-nerves when my kids are sick (and I can't get hold of our local physician). Brandon is known to our six children as our funny friend from a town in Louisiana with a funny name (Trout), who sends them funny Southern books (*A Cajun Night Before Christmas* and *A Texas Night Before Christmas*). Over the years, I have jokingly told the kids not to feed Brandon bacon because bacon would make him oink and squeal uncontrollably due to the fact that he has a pig valve in his heart (true fact! ☺). I thank God for Brandon's friendship on a personal level, and for the way he blesses my entire family and others through his kindness, compassion, and excellent medical practice.

I know you'll enjoy reading about his incredible life and how his and Jeremy's friendship grew into an unbreakable brotherhood. Some of it you won't believe because the apparent random coincidences seem improbable. But, of course, nothing is impossible or random with God. Get ready to laugh, to cry, and to find yourself in a new state of belief—or disbelief! Brandon's story isn't average or ordinary because Brandon isn't ordinary. He's extraordinary. He believes that God loves him, and he believes that God loves you, too. He's a brilliant medical doctor who loves people, saves lives, comforts thousands—and knows that only the Great Physician could have written the story you are about to read. Enjoy!

—Kirk Cameron
ACTOR & PRODUCER

FOREWORD

Is there an order to the universe? I guess so, because otherwise the story of Brandon is one in a random billion. Among the greatest gifts in my life of entrepreneurial philanthropy have been the people I have been privileged to meet. None better than this extraordinary man, Dr. Brandon Lane Phillips. Our Starlight Foundation granted his wish to visit the set of *Growing Pains* in the 1980s, when he was a little boy battling heart problems and a poor medical prognosis. In founding Starlight, there was nothing more complicated in our ambition than to bring happiness to children and their families saddened by their medical condition. We put the child in charge and gave them the steering wheel—control and agency amid an otherwise disempowering and bewildering array of tubes, tests, surgeries, and sterile rooms. So it was that Brandon got a Starlight boost of self-esteem by meeting the stars of his favorite show. But who could have known that this was to be a gift that would go on giving for over three decades? And who could have known that the little boy with a defective heart would grow up to become a leading cardiologist? Our world is mysterious, but, for me, often wonderful to behold. I am humbled and delighted that we could help Brandon find his destiny. And if we were channeling some higher force, what an honor!

—Peter Samuelson
STARLIGHT CHILDREN'S FOUNDATION COFOUNDER

PREFACE

I was led down a darkened hallway through a heavy studio door, and onto a Hollywood soundstage. Overhead, there was scaffolding containing what looked like hundreds of lights. *Does it really take this much light to make the actors look good?* I puzzled, staring upward, my mouth gaping open. The cameras on floor dollies: there were three—no, four—pointed at the set. They illuminated the home that was as familiar to me as my own country home just outside of Jena, Louisiana.

The Seaver family home only had three walls, though, facing bleachers that could probably seat three hundred audience members. I stared in disbelief; I couldn't believe it was the real thing. The blue carpet runner running up the staircase leading to nowhere. The tuba filled with cattails at the base of the steps. The angular wooden beams. Out the open front door was a painted backdrop; I squinted at it, thinking that it looked much more realistic on television. Everything was so much smaller than it appeared on TV—the sets, the props, even the actors, who I could see practicing last-minute lines off to the side.

The production assistant continued to lead us into the kitchen of ABC's sitcom *Growing Pains*. I was an eighties kid, and the show, which ran from 1985 to 1992, was my favorite. Each week I'd excitedly plant myself on the shag rug in the living room the moment it began, munching on popcorn and staring up into the TV screen. What *Lassie* or *Gilligan's Island* might have meant to kids of past generations, that's what *Growing Pains* was for me. Dr. Jason Seaver, a psychiatrist and new stay-at-home dad thanks to his wife Maggie's new reporting job, took care of kids Mike, Carol, and Ben. Mike was a cool-kid slacker and ladies' man, Carol was shy and interested mainly in books, and Ben was rambunctious and looked up to his older brother's shenanigans. The series followed their adventures and misadventures as the kids navigated growing up and their parents tried to keep them out of trouble—but above all, they cared for one another and always had each other's backs.

And there I finally was in the Seaver kitchen, a room that had been filled with so many hilarious conversations. The breakfast table, where teenage Mike Seaver often perched backward in his chair. The center island where brainy Carol always leaned, book in hand, rolling her eyes at her brothers from behind bright-red Sally Jessy Raphael glasses. The sink where Jason and Maggie argued good-naturedly about the kids.

How cool would it be to have a stay-at-home psychiatrist father like the one Alan Thicke played? To have a glassed-in greenhouse in your kitchen? To have older siblings like Mike and Carol? Ben Seaver had everything I wanted. I envied Jeremy Miller, who played Ben. He was my age, but he seemed to have everything I did not. He had a father who lived at home, a fun older brother to get into all kinds of trouble with, and a happy ending to his problems each week. I wanted to be him—or at the very least, get closer to him.

My real life seemed a constant parade of more challenging

growing pains—heart-related doctor visits, medical procedures, surgeries, and darker family struggles. There was no studio audience to "aww" every time I was treated for my heart condition, Tetralogy of Fallot.

Tetralogy of Fallot is a rare and complex, lifelong heart condition. The name of the condition refers to a wide spectrum of pathology, so patients can experience varying degrees of severity, and the condition can be complicated by a number of different factors. However, all patients share the problem that the blood vessel leaving the heart to take blood to the lungs is narrowed, disrupting the direction of blood flow and sending deoxygenated blood out to the brain and other structures. The risks were so serious that when I was eleven years old the Starlight Children's Foundation, an organization that had worked since the early 1980s to brighten the lives of seriously ill children and their families, had chosen to grant my wish to meet Ben Seaver and his entire TV family. I wanted to walk through the Seavers' living room, sit at the Seavers' dinner table, and just be one of the gang for a day. When they finally called and announced that my wish would be granted, I whooped with excitement. Mama and I would fly to Burbank, California, and be picked up and driven to the *Growing Pains* set on the Warner Brothers studio lot.

Little did I know how much the trip would affect my life. The Starlight wish set into motion the idea that if I could go from Jena to Hollywood, I could go from despair to hope, from an adolescent death sentence to the fulfilling life I have today as a pediatric cardiologist, treating children with the same heart problems that have consumed my family and me since the day I was born.

Little did Jeremy Miller know how much my wish would affect his life, too. My wish upon a star was the first time our lives intersected—and it would not be the last.

PART I

WISHING FOR IT ALL

CHAPTER ONE

OPEN-HEART SURGERY
FOR THE BABY

At 11:00 p.m., Mama shot up in bed. I was causing her some mean labor pains. My parents scrambled out of bed, pulling on their clothes and grabbing the neatly packed suitcase next to the door. They piled my sleepy thirteen-year-old sister, Brenda, into the car and dropped her at an aunt's house along the way. With my mother's shooting pains growing worse, my father floored it onto the highway—until he was pulled over by the Louisiana State Police for speeding. They finally arrived and after only two hours of labor—and very close on the heels of the doctor who hurriedly made his way into the delivery room—I arrived.

Back then parents normally didn't know the sex of a child before its birth. Mama learned I was a boy when the doctor who had just helped to bring me into the world exclaimed, "Oh, look! It's a little Kojak!" My tiny bald head gleamed and my face was scrunched into a stony glare. It was the first and only time I've been likened to Telly Savalas.

Mama had been only eighteen when she had Brenda. The focus of all my parents' attention, she'd had the ideal childhood—water skiing, attending stock car races, riding minibikes, camping, and participating in lots of adventures with Mama and Daddy and our extended family. She finally had to rise to the challenge, though, and make room for me.

I'm sure Mama would have preferred to have had her children closer in age. That said, neither thirteen years nor all the time my parents spent trying to have another baby after Brenda could prevent the two of us from becoming the best of friends. From the beginning Brenda thought the sun rose and set on me. It wasn't long before I felt the same about her. She was my "sissy," my "honey bunny." She took care of me when my parents were at work, and she saw to my every need. When I was plagued with sleeplessness and nightmares as a young child, the only way I could find sleep was by crawling into her bed.

In a lot of ways Mama's pregnancy with me had been just like her pregnancy with Brenda. Sure, she was in her early thirties. There was no planned baby shower for what would be the last grandchild on her side of the family. But everything else seemed normal. Mama didn't work outside of the home during either of her pregnancies. Daddy wanted her to be a homemaker and he entrusted her to raise their children without stress. The stay-at-home mom arrangement was standard for most families back then, and "normal" was exactly how Mama's life had been until the moment I arrived.

I entered the world in silence.

Mama waited for it with her heart pounding, but I didn't make a sound. After a moment the doctor and nurses began to whisper among themselves. Mama panicked at the thought of how quickly Brenda's cries had filled the room. Before she could utter any words, though, I released a howl that flooded the room with relief. She tried to bury her anxiety in the back of her mind.

For two days she lay in the hospital bed and kept her questions to herself as doctors ran tests on me. When the time finally came for discharge, my physician told Mama there was a small possibility that I might have a little hole in my heart.

"I *think* he'll do fine," he tried to assure her.

There didn't seem to be much Mama could do but wait. She thought about my condition alone in the hospital room.

Brenda couldn't wait for me to come home so that she could hold me whenever she wanted. I weighed a little more than six pounds, an average-sized baby who at that point didn't particularly look like anyone in the family. I cried a lot and often appeared fretful. Most worrisome for Mama was the tinge of blue that started to appear in my coloring after we arrived home. Brenda still remembers my ten tiny little blue fingers and toes. Even at thirteen she could tell that something was very wrong. Mama took me back to the hospital but they couldn't seem to pinpoint anything, so the doctors recommended that I have additional tests. My parents took me the 130 miles to state-of-the-art Baton Rouge General Medical Center.

Dr. Clifton T. Morris Jr. was the specialist in pediatric cardiology who took over my care. Even before testing, Mama was devastated at the thought of heart trouble. She'd had a cousin whose child with heart problems died soon after she was born. The family referred to her in whispers as the "blue baby." She'd also had an adult cousin who underwent open-heart surgery and was never able to get off the heart-lung machine before dying young.

The results of the testing added my name to our family's list of members with heart complications. Dr. Morris diagnosed me with Tetralogy of Fallot, a rare condition involving a combination of four heart defects present at birth. These defects cause oxygen-poor blood to flow out of the heart and into the rest of the body, leaving infants and children with blue-tinged skin.

Mama had waited so long for another baby. She had diligently collected the things she knew I would need, dusting off Brenda's old high chair and crib. My extended family had showed their love for me and my parents by sharing clothes and toys for me to play with. Although she and Daddy had the physical things I would need, neither had the emotional reserve for the condition that would ultimately define my life.

Dr. Morris delivered the news about my problematic heart with hope. He said that he had faith it could be corrected so that oxygen-rich blood would begin flowing to my extremities again. The heart-lung machine had been invented in 1953, and by this time, doctors were comfortable using it on people of all types. Operations performed on children with my condition were generally successful, though open-heart surgery didn't really become the standard of care for infants until the 1980s. By "successful," I mean that children would live through their operations and experience some improvement. While they might need more surgery or lifelong follow up in many cases, and often would never be able to "compete physically with other children," as Dr. Vargo put it, the surgeries could still give them an improved quality of life.

For more than thirty years these types of surgeries required a child to be about twenty pounds and at least two years old. As a result, it wasn't unusual for families to be told to wait. Dr. Morris recommended my surgery be performed after my seventh birthday. In the meantime, I would undergo regular x-rays and ECGs that would keep tabs on how my heart was progressing.

Every three to six months my parents would trek from Jena to Baton Rouge. They never complained and I am grateful for that. My parents were committed to making sure I was healthy even if it meant time away from home and work. My father was present throughout all that was going on with me, although his lack of initiative forced Mama to make all the decisions. He took time off from work to be exactly where I was for as long as I needed him, even when he lost wages because of it. Mama dreamed of more, a place where I could get the best care possible. Even beyond the boundaries of Louisiana if necessary. One day she received a letter in the mail that made that dream a reality.

Dr. Morris told Mama and Daddy by mail that he would be leaving Baton Rouge to do some additional study at Baylor College of Medicine in Houston. The letter informed them that they would have to find a new pediatric cardiologist to care for me. This cemented the idea in Mama's mind and she immediately suggested that a move to Texas might be good for me, too. She thought Houston could be the place where she would find a larger hospital with state-of-the-art technology and doctors who were better-equipped to help me. My pediatrician recommended she look into Texas Children's Hospital, and that's where, at nearly two years of age, I met Dr. Thomas A. Vargo. He has had a tremendous impact on my life.

From the moment we met he had my best interests at heart. He was quick to propose the radical idea that I should not wait to have open-heart surgery. He believed that the sooner the correction was made the better chance I would have.

This was the first time the stars aligned, so to speak, in my young life. Mama had dreamed of a bigger medical facility with great doctors who could help her son. The place and the faces were yet unknown to her, but she put her faith in her instincts

and found both without a referral or Google or WebMD. Mama
believed she had been led to Dr. Vargo as an answer to a prayer
born in her fragile, aching heart. She had no choice but to put her
complete trust in him.

CHAPTER TWO

FEEBLE HEART,
FRACTURED FAMILY

D r. Vargo recently told me he recalls my parents from their very first meeting. He said he remembers enjoying the ease with which he was able to talk to them about my heart. Mama and Daddy liked Dr. Vargo, too. From the very beginning his demeanor instilled trust.

Mama asked Dr. Vargo if it would be possible for everything to wait until I turned two years old. She wanted me to be able to celebrate my second birthday with family before the surgery. Dr. Vargo was sensitive to the weight of the situation and he agreed. It was only a few months away, anyway. Whatever Dr. Vargo said was good enough for Mama. Never once did she consider seeking another opinion. She relied on the sense of peace she got from him.

But her greatest source of hope came from prayer. Mama says she prayed nearly twenty-four hours a day during that period. When we returned home to wait for my surgery, Mama would lie awake all through the long nights and talk to God. Before she had left Jena, she had taken me to the front of the church, my sister and father alongside her, while the pastor led the congregation in prayer. Standing up there in front of the wooden pews and simple stained-glass windows she had known since childhood, she asked God to take care of me. Tears in her eyes, she gave me back to God and chose to trust Him through whatever was to come.

Several local churches and banks in my local community took up special offerings to pay for some of my medical and travel expenses. Babies with any serious medical condition were rare in Jena, a town of less than 2,500 residents at the time. I believe God moved so many peoples' hearts to help because He was looking out for me. When she heard about the collection Mama cried in gratitude. Then she went right back to the church and prayed for God's intervening hand before and after my surgery, as she would for all my procedures after that.

The only question now was who would do the surgery. Dr. Vargo wanted to leave the decision up to my parents. It was important that they maintain some sense of control over what was in fact an uncontrollable situation. But neither Mama nor Daddy knew of anyone in the field, so they were open to suggestions. Without hesitation, Dr. Vargo recommended Dr. Denton Cooley, a cardiothoracic surgeon who was steadily gaining a great reputation around the country for his work on babies and infants, to do the surgery.

In 1979, there were significant risks involved in doing an operation on such a young heart. Fortunately, Dr. Cooley had proven he could beat the odds. He was a world-famous surgeon credited with performing the first implantation of a completely artificial heart. He had also founded the Texas Heart Institute. He was surgeon in chief at the time of my surgery and would go on to serve in this position until 2014.

Mama purchased a book about Dr. Cooley from the hospital gift shop. She kept the book for decades and presented it to me when I received the Young Alumnus of the Year Award at Louisiana Tech in 2006. Mama bought the book because she had faith I would make it through, and she wanted me to know one day the magnitude of the man who had performed my first open-heart surgery. Little could she imagine that I would meet him many years later during my residency in that same hospital. Or maybe she could.

As the days ticked by Mama had time to contemplate how much I had grown over the past couple of years and how much I had overcome to do so. I had learned to crawl by scooting along with my head down on the floor as if it were too heavy for me to hold up. I had learned to walk but I took breaks to assume a squatting position when I became tired. And I had learned to love music. My favorite was a record belonging to my sister called "Hot Child in the City." Every day, as soon as Brenda left for school, I would go into her room and somehow, at two years of age, turn on her record player. I'd dance to the lyrics, twisting and turning until I could stand no more and had to squat, a grin spread across my small face. Children often bring toys to the hospital to remind them of home. Brenda's record and record player came with me to Houston. The song was constantly played for me in the children's ICU. It brought a smile to my face even in a hospital bed.

My family had cake and ice cream to celebrate my second birthday. Soon afterward I entered the hospital just in time to celebrate Halloween in the children's ward. The festivities were a pleasant diversion for the family. Brenda made it her responsibility to take me "trick or treating," pulling me around in a wagon from one hospital room to the next.

Three days later Mama carried me through the halls of the hospital to the operating room. She says it felt like a death row inmate's walk to execution. It could very well have been the last moments of her young baby's life.

Dr. Cooley normally performed his daily schedule of surgeries in immediate succession. He only paused to change his gloves, study the patient's chart, and regroup with his staff. After his last operation of the day he would go into the waiting room to individually brief the families. For parents and loved ones this meant an agony of waiting. Dr. Cooley charged his nurses with leaving the operating room periodically to keep the patients' loved ones informed.

Once I went into surgery Mama and Daddy didn't see me again until several hours later, at about 2:00 a.m. Parents were always the first to be allowed in the recovery room. Brenda, Aunt Deana, and my grandmothers would have to wait a few hours more to see how I was doing.

They rushed in, bodies frozen in tension, and leaned over the bed. "Love Mama," I said, my eyes barely open. My mom's heart broke, but it also eased her fears.

I opened my eyes and then said the same thing. "Love Mama."

The surgery had been a success, and I was soon moved from recovery to adult ICU, where there were lots of adults and many beds. Every time Mama entered the room, she got a chill at seeing her little baby in a big bed with tubes coming out all over his body. When she enveloped my hands in her own, they were ice cold.

Mama tensed up and brought this to the doctor's attention. No one had told her that it was necessary for my temperature to be lowered. Hypothermia had been used to arrest my heart during surgery. Doctors have since found better, safer ways to stop the heart for surgery.

I stayed in adult ICU for three more days before being transferred to a bed in the children's ICU. I was in the hospital for a total of three weeks. I developed pneumonia. In response the staff used clap therapy, which involves hitting a patient's back to help clear their lungs. They also instructed me to walk up and down the halls to keep air flowing through my lungs. I walked, but on my toes. Mama assumed it was due to the IV lines placed into my feet, but would be surprised to see that this walk persisted even after the IV lines were removed.

One day, I was taken back into surgery for a leaking patch. Tetralogy of Fallot patients have a hole in the wall between the lower two chambers of their heart. A patch had been sewn into my heart to seal the hole, but it was now leaking, enabling blood to flow across the middle. Mama had gone back to the hotel across the street where the family was staying to wash some clothes. When she got back, she heard from Daddy and my grandmothers that I was back in surgery. She became nearly hysterical, imagining all the things that could have happened to me while she was loading clothes into a hotel dryer. From that day on, she never left the hospital. She just sat there, exhausted, wearing the same dirty clothes, day in and day out. The rest of my extended family sat alongside her in the hospital—waiting, worrying, and wearing themselves out.

The family was staying at a Holiday Inn located directly across the street from the hospital. My grandmothers, aunt, and cousin all stayed in one room. Mama and Daddy spent the night in the hospital with me in what was known as a family room during surgery. My family's pastor, Brother Sexton, was there.

Brenda had come for a whole two weeks to be with me, without hesitation, even though it put her ten consecutive years of perfect school attendance in jeopardy.

My first open-heart operation would be the only one we would all be together for. Daddy became convinced that with just one surgery all my health problems had been taken care of—and that it was time to move on.

CHAPTER THREE

Unexpected Best Man Duties

F amilies dealing with a sick child often find themselves dealing with divorce, as well. After the surgery is over and the
critical period of recovery concludes, the possibility of normalcy
appears almost attainable. It is at this point that the typical family
can splinter. My family was nothing if not typical.

Daddy had sat me down on the couch the afternoon of my
fifth birthday and dropped a bombshell: "Son, I won't be living
here starting tomorrow. I'm leaving."

Within minutes I had spread the news to Mama. She was
shocked. She hadn't seen it coming even though she recalled how
some six weeks earlier she'd noticed strange things going on.

My constant health problems had taken a toll on us all. From
the moment I entered the world my well-being had become
everyone's central concern. Mama was researching, trying to
make my sickness go away; Daddy worked hard to support
me by providing for the family. Brenda and my cousin Melissa

would take me to town whenever I asked to get an ice cream. (One particular tale has me riding along in a Jeep by the river near my Aunt Deana's houseboat when I was only three years old. The joy ride ended when we got stuck in the mud, which caused us to return home later than planned, and we had a lot of explaining to do to my worried mother.) Parents of children with congenital heart disease experience high levels of distress and hopelessness, which trickle through the family, often putting a strain on relationships and forcing young children to grow up faster than they should.

I blamed myself for my parents' separation. It took years to realize that their problems were bigger than my heart defect. Daddy's ability to stay faithful, or just stay, had proven wanting even before I was born. Mama was his second of what would eventually be four wives—all wed with promises of "happily ever after," and all divorced except for one.

Daddy's first wife was named Jeanette. She's the mother of my brother, Jerry Glen. Their marriage unraveled when she found out that my father was seeing another woman. He often insisted he had to work overtime, but his paycheck never reflected it. Then, when a couple of relatives confirmed that he was indeed running around town with a barmaid, she knew it was over. (For the sake of clarity, Mama was not the barmaid.)

Daddy didn't deserve a second chance according to Miss Jeanette. She was willing to raise Jerry Glen alone. Fortunately she remarried a man who had no trouble staying put, which gave Jerry Glen a great father to admire.

Jerry Glen didn't even meet our dad until he was fifteen years old. In a town of less than 3,000 people, with our houses being just a few miles apart, it took my paternal grandfather's funeral to get the estranged father and son together. Miss Jeanette made a point of never allowing anyone to say anything bad about Daddy in Jerry Glen's presence. She also encouraged her son to continue to have a relationship with Daddy's side of the family. For that reason, he would see our paternal grandparents along with a few of our aunts and uncles a couple of times a year.

In 1976, a year before I was born, our grandfather's last request was for everyone to attend his funeral. By "everyone" it was clear who he meant. Miss Jeanette said it would have to be Jerry Glen's decision as to whether or not he would go. My brother really wanted to know our dad so he went to the funeral. He gave himself the opportunity to meet his father and begin forging a relationship that would grow stronger with time. Daddy became a part of his life and then the lives of his children. Still, Jerry Glen would never call him "Dad," and Daddy would never say the words "I love you" to him—though he tried to show it in other ways.

My relationship with my father mirrored his with Jerry Glen in some ways. I could feel guilty and dwell on the idea that he left the family because statistics show that a majority of marriages break up when there is a sick child. But I would only be half right. Mama thought it had a lot to do with his feeling that he wasn't needed. From the start she became responsible for most of the decisions regarding my health. He chose to work overtime instead, trying to support me in other ways. He seemed lost in the doctor's office because he was not as well-read in the medical sciences as she was. Often he seemed to just stand on the sidelines.

Brenda agrees with Mama's assessment and takes it a step further. To her, our dad didn't know what to do with both a sick child and another who had found herself in trouble. Brenda got pregnant with her first child at seventeen, just before my father left. She was young and unwed. Together our situations made a perfect storm that put a strain on Daddy. When Mama went from being concerned with me to being just as worried about Brenda, there seemed, in his mind, to be no place for him.

That's when he strayed from his marriage to Mama. He started telling her that he had to work late. Other times he'd say he was visiting my uncle who was sick in the hospital. Perhaps this is the closest he came to telling her the truth. He *was* at the hospital—spending lots of time with a nurse.

Though he had strayed in his first marriage, everyone was blindsided by Daddy's infidelity and his decision to leave. Mama probably would have stayed with him if he had chosen to come back those first few months. For Daddy, there was no turning back. I'll never know whether he felt he'd made a mistake, but once he had committed to it he had to follow through. He initially denied the affair. But a day after he left, Brenda saw his car parked at the hospital and talked Mama into going down and confronting him about his affair. The ugly scene that followed led to other painful arguments that splintered the family further. The fights culminated in another early-morning confrontation at the hospital in which my father had both Brenda and my mother arrested, offering to drop the charges against Brenda only if she got on her knees and begged for forgiveness. The anger and animosity in my family had finally boiled over.

Brenda believes that over time Daddy became a totally different person. As she became more protective of Mama he seemed to turn on her more and more. Daddy married the new nurse, Stevie, almost immediately, and treated her as though she was more important than we were. And yet he only stayed with her for about a year before moving on. He'd soon meet Sue, the local Avon lady, who ultimately became his fourth and final wife.

When I was in the third grade Brenda unexpectedly picked me up from Mama's house and drove me to Daddy's wedding to Sue. I did not know he was getting married. I also did not know I was to be his best man. Sue's daughter served as her bridesmaid, and her son gave her away. They had a ready-made wedding party with their children from previous marriages!

I did not know how or if Daddy's new family would affect my relationship with him. I'd enjoyed visiting with Sue and her children. Her son was a year younger than me. His birthday was three days after mine so we'd celebrate together and ride bikes around town. One Christmas he and I rode bikes to a home nearby his house and marveled at the decorations and mini candy canes on their tree.

I didn't realize they would become a more permanent fixture and further decrease the one-on-one time I would spend with my father; at that moment, I didn't really know what marriage meant. I was unaware of the changes that would come in my relationships with both my father and Sue.

The wedding was at their new country home about ten miles outside of Jena, down a mile-long gravel road. It was a double-wide trailer on about forty acres of land. They referred to it lovingly as "Circle P Ranch." Brenda's husband and boys were also at the wedding; though I was confused about what was to come, and a bit perplexed by my best man duties, I thought the wedding was fun.

***

Shortly after Daddy's marriage to Sue, Mama received a letter from "Lucy." Mama didn't know a Lucy, but she did recognize the handwriting to be Grandma Rachel's. Grandma Rachel, my dad's mother, often used the name to refer to her grandkids when she couldn't readily think of their actual names. "Lucy" had written to reassure Mama that Daddy's new wife was going to take good care of me whenever I was in his custody. While it was unclear to Mama if Grandma was truly trying to reassure her or just trying to reassure herself, what seemed certain was that Daddy's "new family" would be safe—and resembled the one he had left behind. The letter noted that his new wife, like Mama, first had a daughter and then a son. Sue also had three brothers and a younger sister, just like Mama did. Funny how the wanderer seemed to seek the family he'd given up.

Things were fine, on the surface, when I was at my father's new house. There were many things I liked about Sue. As the local Avon lady she took time on her appearance. She rolled her hair in curlers and applied makeup carefully to accentuate her beauty mark. She was a talented cake decorator and made me a wonderful clown cake for my birthday. She was attentive and even boiled the extra toothbrush she had on hand for me because I was afraid of germs.

I would play Scattergories and watch movies with her children. Her son liked to play basketball with his cousins. I was in good health, needing to go in for a checkup only once every two years, but I still lacked coordination, and I often sat these games out. But he and I enjoyed riding four-wheelers and bikes together during my visits.

Even when Daddy was home he was busy. He built shelving to go into Sue's office. He built a wood fence around the house. He milked their cow every day. Daddy had a great sense of humor; he once told me, "Pull the cow's tail if you want chocolate milk." We would gather eggs together, washing them and packing them in cartons to sell at the local store. I got twenty-five cents for each carton sold, and cracked up at the sign in the store that read "homegrown eggs."

But Daddy's restless, wandering, and often distant spirit couldn't help but have an effect on me. I focused on what I was missing when I wasn't there—especially when I was alone. *What was Daddy doing?* I would wonder.

I also felt resentment over the place Sue had taken in his life. She began to say unkind things about me just out of earshot. I became defensive and angry and began to fire back with insults about her or my father. He tried uncomfortably to force us to get along. Once when my friend Jarred was coming over for a sleepover, Daddy made a push to get me to call Sue "Mama." It seemed to me he was trying to play happy family, which felt like a slap in the face. I stepped up boldly, right in front of Jarred, and told him, "I have a Mama. I don't need another." Sue turned and walked from the room, tight lipped.

After the long weekend, I asked Mama how she thought I should refer to Sue. We talked through my complicated feelings and settled on "This is my Daddy and his wife, Sue."

These were also tough times financially. Mama describes my childhood after Daddy left as a three-ring circus that lasted for thirteen years. When Daddy and Sue married, Sue became the one to send the monthly check for child support and alimony. When she sent the first check, she signed it, "Mrs. Jerry G. Phillips." This upset Mama, because it was how she used to sign her checks when she'd been married to Daddy. Before sending it to the bank, Mama took a pen and added "IV" after the signature before cashing it at the bank, a small dig at the woman who had replaced her. Soon, the checks began to come signed "Mrs. Jerry Phillips." She had dropped the "G," no doubt having seen a copy of the check.

Daddy had been a good provider before he left, but his departure changed even the ways he cared for us monetarily. He felt that the child support and alimony he paid were enough. He fought back against extra expenses or anything he felt we didn't "need." The judge, who from the start seemed to favor Daddy's side of the story, decided that Mama was capable of paying for certain things the family needed. He believed the small part-time job gauging wells in the local oil fields held by Daddy would be perfect for Mama and would give him a break from some of his financial responsibilities.

Mama had to approach the owners of the wells to see if they would be agreeable to having her perform the work. To have to rely on part-time oil field work wasn't easy. It was difficult physically. After a year of doing it, she quit to take a job at the local Dairy Queen. There she worked alongside Brenda until she was able to submit papers for a civil service job working with children with special needs. In spite of the judge's decision, the divorce decree, or even Daddy's lack of support, Mama always found a way to take care of us. It took countless hours of hard work and determination. She scraped together enough to feed us, clothe us, and even to provide me with special opportunities like a class trip to Washington, DC. (My father, in contrast, gave me twenty dollars and asked me to buy him a souvenir with it, and grumbled that he didn't see any need in me "gallivanting off to Washington.")

Years after the divorce, the attorney who had represented my father was running for a position as the local judge. He stopped by Mama's home to campaign. He didn't even get to finish introducing himself before Mama quipped, "I wouldn't vote for you if you were running for dog catcher."

He started to explain that he would have done the same thing for her if she had come to him first, but this only further upset

Mama. "It shouldn't matter who came first. It should only matter what is right."

I saw how Mama handled things, how she bore it with a smile even through the physical and emotional toll it took on her. I became more and more disappointed in Daddy. I wanted to forge a relationship with him to try to understand why he would do what he had done. Yet I often found myself frustrated by his games. When my parents first separated I would call Daddy at home. He'd pick up only to disguise his voice, tell me I had the wrong number, and then hang up on me. When I called back I'd get a busy signal. Daddy had taken his phone off the hook, leaving me to spend the next hour trying to call him back. Even today, my instinct is not to leave people voice mails out of a deep-seated fear that they will never call me back.

Daddy blamed his lack of involvement in my life on work the times that I confronted him about it. I knew he wasn't always on the job even when he said he was, though. A person can only be at work for so many hours—and that's coming from a doctor.

Once I called him because I wanted to spend time with him. He declined, saying he was working out of town, but I felt it was a lie. Sensing where he was—at his stepson's basketball game—I asked Mama to take me to the school.

"No. Sorry," she replied, eyeing me warily. "It's late. I'm tired."

"All right. I'll walk there."

She had no room to refuse. It was dark and she didn't want me walking alone. She sighed and drove me to the school. I walked into the gym and discovered with a sinking feeling that I was right. Daddy was sitting on the bleachers, watching the game.

I mounted the bleachers, heart heavy, and took a seat next to him. He looked over at me, surprised, then cleared his throat and looked away.

"You lied to me."

Our pastor was sitting nearby; Daddy seemed to look over at him for help. He offered none, turning his eyes back to the game. I let him know that I was disappointed and hurt before I left.

When I got back in the car, Mama asked me if Daddy had been there. "Yes," I replied, and stared straight ahead. We drove home in silence.

There were other instances in which Daddy let me down. He didn't show up for one of my more important medical procedures. Dr. Vargo had recommended a heart catheterization. A catheterization is a diagnostic procedure in which a catheter is guided up into the heart to enable doctors to measure the pressure in the heart, take blood samples to assess the blood's oxygen saturation throughout the heart, and inject contrast media to better outline the heart's chambers and vessels. While it's not exactly a surgery, it is invasive, and I was afraid. Daddy knew the time and the day, and he promised to be there. He didn't show up. I was beside myself. I cried, saying that he had lied to me. I was agitated and could not be comforted. Mama decided the best thing was for her to lie down on the hospital gurney alongside me and quiet me down until the medication kicked in. All the while, she whispered that it would be okay. Eventually it was. A day or two later Daddy showed up. He didn't apologize—he almost never apologized.

Sometimes it was a struggle to get Daddy to do what he should have done willingly. The judge told him he'd be responsible for any of my medical bills that the insurance company didn't pay. But although he had the resources to pay he seemed to find each new procedure unnecessary; in his eyes, I should have been cured after the first procedure.

Even the paperwork presented difficulties. Daddy's company

changed insurance providers from time to time in order to try to get the best deal. Whenever a change happened it would always be a big ordeal for Mama to get the new policy numbers. It just wasn't among my dad's priorities. Once Brenda had to go to Daddy's office for the numbers while Mama and I waited to be seen for a checkup in Houston. Daddy's boss was very surprised that my dad was not with us since he had taken off work specifically to take me to the doctor. Brenda let him know that Daddy wasn't taking care of business at home.

Daddy found out what Brenda had done when his boss called him on the phone. Although he'd brought it upon himself, he was embarrassed and incredibly angry at Brenda. They didn't speak for nearly six months afterward.

Daddy thought my heart troubles ended with my very first heart surgery. That was wishful thinking on his part. The arguments over insurance happened because he thought my checkups were unnecessary. He thought my heart had been repaired. Stevie, his third wife, occasionally hooked me up to a heart monitor when Daddy and I would visit her at work. The test was like the ECG that was performed each time I would see Dr. Vargo; it was painless, I loved electronics, and I got to keep the tracing! But it didn't help my case with Daddy. While a keen observer may have noticed a slight aberration in my results, my heart was beating in a normal rhythm so Stevie deemed me healthy and my father believed her. It wasn't long before he got it in his head that he was paying for Mama and me, and sometimes Aunt Deana and Brenda, to take a family "vacation" whenever I went for a doctor's visit in Houston, especially if I had to stay overnight in the hospital. To prove him wrong, Mama would ask him to come with us, but he'd always say he had to work. The man was a very busy worker.

Daddy would often berate Mama for choosing the most expensive medical care for me. His response was to threaten to stop paying the policy so my health benefits would be dropped. When Dr. Vargo heard about this he told Mama in confidence that he would treat me whether I had insurance or not. It made Mama cry to think a doctor would freely treat her child and to reaffirm that she could trust in him although her trust in my father had failed. Dr. Vargo tried to play down his offer and make her feel less guilty about it. He told her that giving treatment to me without pay would not make or break him. Dr. Vargo expected no thanks or praise. I think he knew what we were going through with Daddy. He understood and this was his way of saying so.

While Daddy was not there for me during some pretty crucial times in my young life, I tried to be there for him. Like Jerry Glen, I wanted to know him. However, I never knew what to expect from someone who was so distant.

My dad's mom once told me that Daddy always wanted a perfect son to follow him around. Unlike his new stepson I was not that boy. I was defective. But so were the people who loved me—and I loved them anyway.

I was not defective, Mama would explain. She'd gather me into her arms. "We all have different strengths and weaknesses—you, your daddy, me, everyone. But you are my smart little boy. What God missed in your heart, he made up for in your head. So you always choose to use it, to think your way through your problems, to believe in yourself."

I chose to have faith and believe she was right.

CHAPTER FOUR

THE DOOGIE IN ME

When I was three I would follow my brother, Jerry Glen, around the house with my toy doctor's kit. I was a regular patient in real doctors' offices and hospitals, so I was an old pro. But it was fun making believe I was on the other side of the stethoscope. My version of "playing doctor" was a lot more literal than that of other kids. I copied my doctor exactly; I would have him take deep breaths when I listened to his back to hear his lungs but was quiet when I listened to his chest to better hear his heart. I was a miniature pretend Doogie Howser quite a few years before the Neil Patrick Harris show caught the nation's attention.

One thing that I couldn't seem to repair was my relationship with my dad. I couldn't even diagnose the problem. There were several barriers that made it nearly impossible to have the kind of father-son relationship that I longed for us to have. Over the years, there were instances that left me questioning if he could be a good parent or even a good person.

The judgments I made about him left a lasting impact. Somehow, my sister and brother were able to mend fences with him in ways I never could. Maybe because they ended up being parents, they were more keenly aware of the grace and skill required to be a parent, which allowed them to see him as more than a disappointment.

It was hard for me to recover from some of the things Daddy did during my childhood to get at Mama. As I entered sixth grade I thought distance had become our barrier. I had been going to school in a different district so my maternal grandmother could watch me while Mama worked nights. I asked to switch elementary schools so that I could spend time with him on the nights when Mama was gone. It took some time—months and months—until he agreed to let me stay overnight. But I hung in there, hoping it would eventually make us closer.

It was a good plan until it backfired. My father started charging babysitting fees to reduce his child support payments. To be clear, Daddy made much more money than Mama. What he had been required to give by the court was barely a hardship for him, but it was a blessing to Mama and our household. Eventually, staying at his house on the nights when Mama worked wasn't an option. I was tired of trying; I didn't want to change schools again. I was left alone at night, which was all I wanted.

After they had been divorced for thirteen years, Daddy chose to take Mama to court and sue her for a property settlement. It was the week of my high school graduation, and I was to be named valedictorian of my class. My father had no concept of how much work had gone into making the day happen. School had been my singular focus for years, representing not only an escape from the pain at home but the possibility of an escape from Jena to a bigger world. I was fiercely proud of being named valedictorian. His timing could not have been worse. The fact that he had chosen to cast a cloud over my graduation upset me, and it stung more that it was once again over money. My entire childhood life had revolved around money—what Daddy gave, what he neglected to give, and what things cost. Daddy was choosing to play games with us, and he was winning; the settlement dredged up years of broken financial issues from my memory.

Even with the finances off the table I didn't have much in common with the man. My condition made it hard to play sports. I would not be able to do the type of physical labor that he had done to get to where he was. Our interests were just not the same. Mama tried to shield me whenever possible from sports at school, and she turned Jerry Glen's offers to hang out like brothers at the lake into a prospect so stressful it wasn't even worth asking about. In surviving my heart defect I'd found myself set apart. There were some things I would never do and others I would completely lose interest in because I couldn't keep up with the others. No one wants to live life sitting in the press box at the Little League baseball fields, keeping the official score book and announcing to the fans in the stands who is on deck to bat.

I never lost the desire to be close to my dad. My escape from the pain was to retreat to my studies. I couldn't wait to get to college and set my sights on higher goals and bigger challenges. I was ready to leave my childhood behind.

I wanted to treat others who had the same heart condition as mine. I vocalized my career goal often, even at a very young age. I wanted to be like Dr. Vargo, my pediatric cardiologist who would later become my mentor, advisor, professor, and ultimately my friend. In some ways he became a replacement for my father as the man I most wanted to emulate.

***

My visits to Texas Children's usually required multiple stops in the hospital. We would start in the clinic and they would tell us where to go for a chest x-ray, ECG, and echocardiogram. Those were standard every visit. Occasionally I would also need a stress test. I would bear with all these tests, frustrated with the other doctor trainees who were performing them and anxious to see Dr. Vargo again. Once all of the tests were complete I would meet with him to review the results.

I grew up adoring Dr. Vargo because he always made me feel like I was more than just a patient. He called me "friend" during my appointments. If I was in the hospital and he missed me on his rounds, he left notes saying he had stopped by—even if they were scrawled on a piece of paper towel from the dispenser in the room. He would lie down alongside me to review my x-ray film; once he got tangled in the blood pressure cuffs and dragged them all down the hall with him. These tiny gestures made him seem down-to-earth and approachable even in the face of his incredible professionalism. He made me feel as though I was always on his mind.

He made such a great impression that I not only wanted to be a pediatric cardiologist, I also wanted to work with him. As time went on I began to look forward to my checkups, so I could barrage Dr. Vargo with lots of questions about my career goals. He always took the time to throw out wisdom that would stick with me, such as, "A physician's bedside manner is just as important as how smart he or she is."

I even wrote to him between visits to share news about my life and request help with special school projects related to medicine. Unlike my father, he always replied.

CHAPTER FIVE

THE PRESURGERY
PHONE CALL

In 1989, I was eleven years old and received a gift that would change my life forever. Starlight Children's Foundation is a global organization founded in 1982 by Peter Samuelson, a TV and film producer, and his cousin, actress Emma Samms. Other wish-granting programs at the time, such as the Make-A-Wish Foundation, focused on terminally ill kids. Starlight was different because it granted wishes to critically and chronically ill children, too. These fine folks granted me a wish.

This distinction comforted Mama, who initially reacted negatively to an organization selecting me for something that she thought was meant for a dying child. She gave permission only after I clarified the Starlight folks' mission for her. She had long ago decided I would survive my heart condition. On the surface, I was doing well. Yet I was still plagued by thoughts that I would die young. I also feared more pain, more surgery, and a growing inability to keep up with the other kids physically. Processing these feelings without confiding in anyone left me irritable and emotional. Our home was occasionally wracked with tension. My mother was frustrated at my emotional standoffishness and singular focus on my studies. After my emotions boiled over, I retreated to my room wounded after a bitter statement or angry glance from her. I knew it was difficult for her to deal with my situation. She had to acknowledge the seriousness of my condition to grant her permission for me to receive the wish, which I know was hard for her. By comparison, Dr. Vargo showed no hesitation. He thought my receiving a wish could only be a positive thing.

Starlight Children's Foundation arose out of the desire to create magnificent experiences and memories families could cherish for years to come. The granting of a wish usually started with a phone call from a parent or a doctor on behalf of the sick child. In my case, I initiated the process. Spending time at home alone I had grown accustomed to picking up the phone to get information; when I moved school districts that same year, I had no qualms about calling my new teacher at home to get the school supply list. I had heard briefly about Starlight on a talk show. That encounter had piqued my curiosity, so I called to get more information on exactly what it meant to be *critically or chronically* ill.

The lady on the other end of the telephone politely answered my questions and then asked a few of her own about why I had called. The conversation ended with her asking when Mama would return, because she would like to speak to her. I knew just enough to get excited about the possibility, without it ever occurring to me that maybe I should have waited for a parent to call for me.

Starlight had office locations in only a few cities around the country. Jena, Louisiana, wasn't one of them. My request went to the Los Angeles office, where it landed on the desk of wish coordinator Amy Albin. She called me one Tuesday afternoon soon after I'd arrived home from school.

"If you could go anywhere, meet anyone, or have anything, what would it be?" the kind voice on the phone asked. "Choose something for each of those categories."

I thought for a few moments; I hadn't prepared for anything like this. But then the responses came flooding out. My "anywhere" wish would be a trip to Hawaii. Mama and I had been there a few years earlier to visit Brenda and her family when Brenda's husband was stationed at Schofield Barracks in Oahu. It was a wonderful trip. We visited Pearl Harbor, the Dole pineapple farm, and beautiful Waimea Falls Park. But the best part had been spending time with Brenda, talking and walking from her home to the beach in the sunshine each day. I always knew it to be a place I wanted to visit again.

I could also go to Disneyland, I chattered on. I'd always wanted to go there. My family had been to Disney World when I was four; I vividly remember the electric parade and loving Mickey Mouse so desperately that I cried when he would not come home with me. When we arrived home, Mama had pulled out the encyclopedia and read to me that he was a "fictional character"—he wasn't real. It was my first introduction to the encyclopedia, which became a frequent reference for me as I grew up.

As for my "anything" choice, it would definitely be a Commodore C64 computer. My "anyone" wish would be to meet Jeremy Miller, who played Ben Seaver on *Growing Pains*. I knew I couldn't live his character's life but I could meet the guy who played him, which seemed close enough to give me some insight into his world.

I remember lying in bed praying through tears that God

would do something to prove His love for me. There were times when my life seemed so dark. I rarely if ever fully shared the emotional impact my illness had on me. I was overcome with guilt over my parents' divorce, which I took responsibility for at the time. I desperately wanted my father's approval. Like most people who think no one would understand, I tried to downplay the dark thoughts I had. But they were always there.

Instead of sharing these fears with Mama or Brenda, I expressed my pain to God. His response didn't come instantaneously. Instead, beginning with my wish, a string of events started to fall into place. They answered my cry in ways that seemed at first coincidental and then very much like God. Interestingly, even now, events happen in my life that bring me back to the day of my wish and remind me of God's answer to my prayer.

When I went for my heart checkup in 1989, Dr. Vargo recommended that I have a heart catheterization so that he could better evaluate my heart. I immediately became tearful at the thought of the procedure. I did not want to have any procedure done. I didn't want any reaffirmation that I had a heart problem. I didn't want the pain. I didn't want the risks. I was also terrified of being put to sleep.

As a peace offering, Dr. Vargo mentioned that the hospital was looking for a kid to throw out the opening pitch at an Astros game that evening and he asked if I would like to do it. I reluctantly had to decline. Mama didn't want to stay over in Houston because Brenda was expecting to have her third child soon. Knowing I would miss the opportunity to be on the field with the Astros, I still had to ask Dr. Vargo a question before I left: I wanted to be awake for the procedure instead. He could just use a local anesthetic. I wanted to work with him one day, I pressed, so it was an amazing learning opportunity. He looked surprised but said we could discuss it later.

Brenda's son Logan was born on August 16, 1989. Mama and I were there for his birth and for the revelation that he had been born with a birth defect, a cleft lip and palate. On the surface, you would not think my heart defect and the baby's cleft lip had anything in common, but in reality, we were realizing that "mid-line" defects, or issues that occur along the vertical axis of the body, ran in my family. On my father's side one of my first cousins has since had another child with a cleft lip, and another has a daughter with spina bifida, all considered mid-line defects.

My heart catheterization was scheduled for the next day, so Mama and I had to head to Houston soon after seeing him. I am quite sure it was difficult for Mama to be with me in the hospital in Houston knowing that Brenda was in the hospital in another state with a newborn baby who would inevitably need several corrective surgeries of his own.

On the day of my procedure I found out that Starlight Children's Foundation had decided to grant my wish, clearing the way for me to meet Jeremy Miller. We got the call while at Texas Children's Hospital. The timing couldn't have been more perfect. I had entered the hospital nearly hysterical with fear at another procedure. After Starlight informed me I could have my wish as soon as I recovered, I became emboldened. I begged Dr. Vargo to allow me to be awake during the catheterization. I reemphasized the fact that I wanted to be a pediatric cardiologist and one day work with him, so I should start learning now.

I had never spoken with such confidence about my future before. My certainty made Dr. Vargo agree to use only a local anesthetic for the procedure so that I could witness everything. For other doctors, this may have seemed to be a ridiculous request coming from an eleven-year-old boy. But Dr. Vargo took me seriously. He gave in and used only a local anesthetic for the procedure so I could witness it all.

I remember asking many questions, fascinated by the image of my heart on the screen. It looked just like it did in the x-rays, but now I was looking at the real thing! Eventually Dr. Vargo assigned a nurse to stand with me to help answer my questions. For some images, he had to inject a contrast media to help outline the heart and its blood vessels. I remember the contrast media injections made me feel warm all over and have the urge to urinate.

"You're a brave kid—and one day, you'll be a brave doctor," he remarked afterward. He told me that he had once asked to be awake for a procedure—and then spent the entire time telling the doctors to speak up because he couldn't hear what they were saying. I guess for some people, this method of learning isn't the greatest idea. He chuckled to Mama that I'd had a few more questions than I should have, but all went fine.

The next day I was discharged from the hospital, and Mama and I went to check on Brenda and Logan at the hospital back home. They would be going home soon, once Brenda met with the plastic surgeon who would perform Logan's surgeries. We were very happy to be leaving. When visiting hours were over, we were stopped by security, who tried to detain me in the hospital; we had left Houston in such a hurry that I was still wearing my hospital ID band.

My recovery took less than a month. While I healed and waited for my wish, Daddy surprised me by agreeing to let me stay with him and his family on the nights when Mama worked. Though this arrangement only lasted a couple of weeks, I felt God had finally addressed my prayer to be with him. I couldn't have been happier.

On September 13, Starlight flew Mama, Aunt Deana, and me to Los Angeles. They had booked us a room at the Beverly Hilton Hotel. Aunt Deana joined us on the trip because Mama was a single parent, and Starlight didn't have any problem taking a second person into account when making our travel arrangements. Our itinerary became a combination of wish requests. I would get to meet Jeremy Miller on the Warner Brothers Studios lot, and while we were in Los Angeles we would also visit Disneyland and the Universal Studios theme park. Wish children are typically assigned a wish escort, and Amy Albin was mine. This was a bit out of the ordinary since she normally never associated with the families on this level. She doesn't know how she came to be the one to accompany us; all I know is that my relationship with Amy has lasted to this day.

Amy remembers her first impression of me: a small child with neatly cropped reddish-blond hair, jumping with joy and incredibly excited to have my wish granted. Having done her research, she knew my condition wasn't terminal so that lightened the mood from the start. She also understood that because I came from a small town, a trip to L.A. had the potential of being quite eye-opening for all of us. Amy says she could tell just how much the experience meant to me from the start, and I impressed her with how poised and well-behaved I acted throughout.

As for Mama she was initially a bit skeptical as to how the whole wish thing would work. In the back of her mind she was afraid it was a scam. She didn't want me to get my hopes up only to be disappointed. But the whole thing turned out to be seamless—even better than anyone could have imagined.

When we arrived in Los Angeles the evening before my wish, a lot of things seemed different to us, but we were ready to meet the challenges. We'd expected to feel unsafe there, having heard about gang violence on the news, but the weather was warm and the people all seemed friendly. It was simply odd not to recognize anyone at all, since we knew everyone in Jena and recognized someone everywhere we went back home.

Starlight had rented us a new model Pontiac Grand Prix to drive. It was the first time we'd ever encountered six lanes of traffic, driving up the 405. And speaking of that, why were all of their freeway numbers preceded with the word "the" ("the 405," "the 101," "the 10")? Why did the freeways overlap, like on the new postcard I had bought? How did these motorcycles whiz between lanes, driving right between cars, and how did people navigate this fast-moving and terrifying traffic? It was so baffling—and exciting—to me.

On the first afternoon we struggled to put gas into the Grand Prix for what felt like forever, only to have an attendant come out and tell us the tank was already full. Almost immediately after, a wrong turn on Rodeo Drive resulted in our driving on the sidewalk until we could get turned around. People scattered out of the way, shopping bags in hand, stunned looks on their faces as we flew past a row of palms and off the curb. I'm certain anyone who saw us could hear the theme song to *The Beverly Hillbillies* playing in their head. Soon Mama mastered getting around the city like a pro. She just relied on the GPS of the day—which was a thick Thomas Guide map that came in the form of a spiral-bound two-hundred-page book. The city was huge!

Once on the right side of the road, the first thing we did was head to the International House of Pancakes for breakfast. I had never been to one, but it sounded exotic and global. Up until then, I'd only experienced "continental breakfasts" at motels (dry toast, pastries, and warm milk left out too long), so it felt great to visit this international restaurant. I liked their "funny face" pancakes so much we went back each morning.

We spent the rest of the morning shopping. We wanted to buy something nice to wear—having never been to L.A., we didn't realize how casual it was, and Mama was worried that her blue jeans would not be fit to wear in Hollywood. So we went to the Beverly Center, which to us didn't look like a mall at all. It was more like an office building in the middle of Beverly Hills filled with a bunch of high-end, high-priced stores. Some of the fancy clothing stores with hard-to-pronounce names seemed nearly empty. *What was that nearly naked mannequin advertising?* we wondered. There weren't even any racks of clothes—just soft lighting and new wave music pumping through the speakers. The salespeople seemed totally uninterested in selling us anything— or even acknowledging us, really. Maybe the stores in that mall sold only oxygen?

While in L.A., we also went to Disneyland. I rode the Pirates of the Caribbean, Haunted Mansion, and Splash Mountain repeatedly, shouting with joy. We also toured Universal Studios, where I loved the backlot tour. They even chose a child from the audience to ride on E.T.'s bicycle using a green screen! And we visited Tony Roma's restaurant, where the chef was expecting us and brought out a delicious fried cheese appetizer. I had never had anything like it back home. But in the end, Mama didn't know which ride was wilder—Disneyland's Matterhorn or the L.A. freeways.

When it came time to go to the *Growing Pains* set, she left the rental car at the hotel, and, like the celebrities Starlight made us out to be, we took a limousine to the studio. It was early afternoon when we arrived on the Warner Brothers lot.

Jeremy met me at the limousine when we pulled in. Now

face-to-face, we were two boys, age twelve and eleven, trying to get to know each other. While many wish kids had visited the *Growing* Pains set, I later learned that I was the first kid whose wish was specifically to meet Jeremy and spend the day with him. For that reason, Jeremy was determined to make sure I had fun.

I don't recall our entire first conversation. But I do remember that one of the very first things Jeremy asked me was if I went to church. The question immediately brought me back to my prayer to God. I felt set up in a good way to be exactly where I was—in the midst of my dream wish.

Before the show started taping, my family got the chance to eat with the cast and crew. Mama and Aunt Deana ate with Jeremy's family; Jeremy and I ate with his brother Josh and Alan Thicke's son Robin, the now-famous R&B pop star. We didn't know what to expect, but the cast and crew made us feel at home. Jeremy and I helped ourselves to chicken from the buffet. I was amazed at the amount of fresh fruit and crunchy vegetables available, as I had been since I'd arrived in L.A. We talked about what grade we were in at school, our birthdays, our siblings, and favorite classes and sports.

Mama instantly liked and connected with Kathleen Freeman, a character actress who was playing a small part in that week's episode. She was comical and down-to-earth. She dramatically took a big sniff when she entered the dining area and said, "What's for dinner? Something smells good." They all made us feel more than welcome.

Jeremy and I hung out all afternoon before the taping. We rode bikes and "borrowed" golf carts so we could ride around the studio back lot. Next, we climbed up into a barn that had been featured in the movie *Friday the 13th*. Jeremy warned me about the "cobwebs," a word I'd never heard before, and then revealed his plan to jump out of the barn and into a giant pile of hay. He had to coax me into it, but I was determined not to chicken out, and finally threw myself off the top into the pile, laughing. In the back of my mind, I knew Mama would kill me if she caught me; after all, it had been less than a month since my heart catheterization. But the sheer joy of being a kid in a new world had overcome me. The day was already full before the added bonus of seeing *Growing Pains* being taped live that evening.

It was the "Teach Me" episode from *Growing Pains'* fifth season. We were shown our seats and given special stickers to show we could stay in the building after the taping. I loved seeing the episode taped and the cast called out to talk with the audience afterward. It was magical to see it all happen in real time.

After the show, I spent time alone talking to Kirk Cameron. While his character seemed larger than life on TV, he seemed much smaller and more approachable in person. He had a soft voice and a genuine way of speaking; our conversation seemed so attuned to my situation, and I hung on his every word. He spoke of God's love and the fact that my life had God-given purpose. When I left the set that evening, I remember thinking about my prayer and wondering how Kirk knew what to say to me.

I left the set with a *Growing Pains* script and T-shirt signed by the entire cast. Kirk had signed the shirt, "God bless you."

During the limousine ride back to the Beverly Hilton, sandwiched between Mama and Aunt Deana, I clutched the shirt and thought about my trip. I replayed the conversation I'd had with Kirk in my mind. I mulled over the fact that I'd just met these two heroes. I was struck by a mixed emotion I couldn't explain. I began to cry in the car, but when Mama asked me what was wrong, I couldn't verbalize it. I just couldn't believe all that had happened to me.

Between Kirk and Jeremy, I had been given more than just a wish. I had been given hope.

Ben Seaver was even better in real life than he was on television. If I could visit *Growing Pains* and meet my favorite character, I could do anything. The way I saw it, my trip from Jena, Louisiana, to Los Angeles was a journey that had set me on a new path and changed my life for good.

After we arrived home, I realized that I had managed to leave the set without a single picture with, or even of, Jeremy. The only picture I have with a cast member was taken on set with Kirk when he was talking to me about God. Kirk wasn't who I went to meet; in truth, I didn't even like his character, Mike Seaver. He was older than I was, and he seemed like a troublemaker. But even as a kid, I knew it was not a coincidence that the only photographic proof of my wish was uniquely tied to a conversation that seemed to be an answer to my prayer.

Even when I returned to school, I still felt that anything was possible. I shared photos of my trip for a class presentation and beamed with pride when the other kids exclaimed over my travels in excitement. I began to make all A's in school. I became more focused, maintaining a 4.0 GPA from then through my graduation from Louisiana Tech University. I was full of life because, like Kirk said, I had a future filled with purpose and promise. If I wanted to be a pediatric cardiologist, I could. It was in me, as sure as the heart that God had given me was in me. And maybe that heart didn't have to define my hopes and dreams.

***

Through the years, Mama says that it was hard not to ask, "Why Brandon? Why the sickness?" And then later, "Why did the family have to go through a divorce?" Mama's search for answers led to her understanding that sometimes life goes along so smoothly that we forget we *need* God. After my wish, I could amend that by saying at other times life goes along so smoothly we know that we *have* God.

The connections I made that day on the *Growing Pains* set would ultimately come to last a lifetime despite our different circumstances. Jeremy and I wrote each other for a few years, although we lost contact when the show ended. I often prayed that I would get to see Jeremy and Kirk again. I so believed that it would happen that I would often keep an eye open for them when I would travel.

I made a wish to meet Jeremy Miller when I was just eleven years old. But before that, I said a prayer to God when I was just…low. Now, more than twenty-eight years later, I've learned that the purpose or call that now defines my life came to be when I actually believed that nothing was impossible—all it took was a wish upon a star.

CHAPTER SIX

THE ENCOURAGING WORDS
OF A PASTOR

I used to tease Mama by calling her "one fishy lady" because she'd grown up in Fishville, a tiny community in central Louisiana. It was a popular summer spot for the surrounding area, where lots of families would come out to enjoy the cold creeks and relax at one of the many camp houses located along the numerous rivers and streams. *Divine Secrets of the Ya-Ya Sisterhood*, which was first a book and then a movie starring Sandra Bullock, was based on the area.

My mother had graduated from Pollock High School (which shares its name with a North Atlantic fish), and even though my childhood home was eight miles outside of the town of Jena in the Eden community, our mail was delivered from the post office in Trout, Louisiana.

She was one of five children. But in many ways my grandparents raised two separate families. They had three boys and then waited twelve years to have two girls, about three years apart.

Mama was the older of the girls; her oldest brother was nineteen years her senior. Mama dreamed of being an airline stewardess and getting married. At the time, marriage was pretty much the height of people's aspirations in Fishville. Getting married meant you were a success in the eyes of the community.

At seventeen, Carolyn Jane Wagoner "made it" by walking down the aisle with Jerry Glen Phillips, one week after she graduated. She had met my father when she was a junior in high school through friends at the skating rink. Daddy was twenty-one, living in Jena, Louisiana, and working in the oil fields. Brenda was born a year later, and then thirteen years after that I came along. Brenda and I followed Mama's family tradition of being raised in two completely different households. Although we had the same parents our childhoods were quite different.

For almost twenty years Mama had lived a TV-style American Dream. It was very *Happy Days*. She had a loving husband and wonderful daughter who enjoyed doing almost everything with her. For a long time that is how it seemed it would always be. Then I was born with a heart problem. Brenda got pregnant out of wedlock. Daddy moved Mama aside for another woman. The family and her life would never be the same. Mama was part of the ever-widening group of divorced women in America raising children. Like passing from light into darkness, Mama went from being a very devoted wife, mother, and homemaker to a divorced single mom whose main focus was taking care of her children while personally doing whatever she could to keep a roof over our heads.

There was never a good time for Daddy to leave the family. His walking out on us emotionally and financially had forced Mama into the role of a fighter. Her opponents were the legal profession when it came to her divorce from Daddy, the medical profession in regards to my health problems, and even academia, which would later demand her attention on my behalf. Throughout it all she also suffered tremendous loneliness. Mama has said that in some ways it would have been easier if Daddy had died—death wouldn't have marred her good memories of their marriage the way his leaving did.

When the original jobs at the oil field and Dairy Queen didn't work out, Mama had to find a full-time job that paid decent money while allowing her to maintain her role as my primary caregiver. After leaving the Dairy Queen in Jena, Mama worked as a security officer in a male Louisiana state prison facility in Pineville, Louisiana. Some of the inmates had been incarcerated for ten years or longer, and many were working to get back into society through a minimum security work program. Mama liked her job; she never had any trouble doing it because she wasn't above asking for help when she needed it. I like to think this is a trait I inherited from her.

The commute required nerves of steel, though. Pineville was some thirty miles away from home, and Mama worked the night shift up to five alternating days per week. Because of this schedule, Mama found it necessary to enroll me in a school outside of our parish and enlist the help of my grandmother, who lived halfway between home and Mama's job. When Mama's workday was done, she would pick me up from Grandma's house before midnight and we would make the fifteen-mile trip home, only to get up before 6:00 a.m. again the next day so I could make it to Grandma's to catch the school bus on time. She would then drive back home to sleep a few more hours before going to work in the afternoon. When I would finish my school day, I would wait at Grandma's until Mama got off work later that evening and the cycle would begin again. Mama was always very adamant that she wanted us to live at *our* house, though; she refused to move, no matter the toll the commute took on her.

I loved spending time with my grandmother. She would sing off-key melodies constantly, infusing the house with joy. I would construct my own bowling alley using two-liter bottles as pins, and she'd often join in the game. Sometimes I'd walk up the hill to play with my distant cousins in the woods. They were a little rougher around the edges, and I was excited by spending time with them, although I didn't always know what they were talking about. I remember one of my female cousins telling a boy that he used "a Band-Aid and contact lens for a jock strap." I remembered the phrase, but it took me a few more years to understand why it was insulting. I would also occasionally walk across the field to visit my great-aunt and great-uncle. He was an engineer. He would talk to me about electronics and math. It was a treat to visit with him.

The house was humble but full of comforting memories. Grandma occasionally made dinner for us, but most of the time I heated up a can of soup and made a grilled cheese sandwich in her toaster oven. Grandma also kept frozen doughnuts and ice cream in her freezer, and there were always apples in her lowest cabinet drawer. Her house didn't have central air or heat. In the winter she put extra covers on the bed. One of the things I loved was getting into a cold bed and moving my legs around to warm up the bed.

My grandfather was still at home when I first started to stay with them, although he was beginning to show signs of Alzheimer's. He raised corn in the field near his home. I remember watching him take his pocket knife and cut corn off the cob to place on a shelf nailed to a tree for the squirrels. Grandpa was a carpenter. The house he'd built for Mama and Daddy was the last house he built, which was part of the reason why Mama didn't want to move.

Mama always kept diligent care of the family home. She was a neat freak—a little OCD, even, before we called it that. She would make me vacuum my stuffed animals regularly to get rid of the dust mites. After Daddy left, Mama's need to maintain a clean and organized house intensified. Mama developed a unique laundry regimen. My white athletic socks were labeled in pairs with a Sharpie marker with a number or letter so each sock would have a distinct mate so that the socks would wear evenly with time. Clothes were washed one item at a time, hung up to air dry, ironed, and then hung in the closet in a plastic bag on a hanger that had been freshly washed in the dishwasher to get the "dust" off of it. Some items, like blue jeans, were hung up inside out to avoid any stray dust mites that could be in the air. I was never quite sure if Mama felt that I needed a sterile environment to protect my heart—or if she was just occupying her mind since her heart had been broken, as well.

***

I often find myself saying it took a village to get me to where I am today. I recognize and appreciate everything Mama did and still does. But in light of the fact that Daddy was absent and she worked full time, there were many people who filled the gap and came to our aid. Aside from Grandma, there was Mama's sister-in-law, my Aunt Janie, and Mama's sister, my Aunt Deana. Aunt Janie always made the best huckleberry cobbler when I visited, and I loved staying with Aunt Deana—she had cable, and we'd watch *Inspector Gadget* together.

Brenda was also a big help to Mama even though she had her

own family. On November 30, 1982, Brenda's first son Jared was born, and I became a very young uncle. In his own way, this little baby made things easier, too. Until Brenda married Jared's dad two years later, she and Mama were single mothers together raising their sons side by side, finding strength and support in each other.

Brenda was my strength and support, too. She'd moved back from Hawaii to Jena, and I would often stay with them on weekends or when school was out, helping with the baby and playing with her older boys. There's so much more that can be said about the uniqueness of our relationship, but for now, it's just important to emphasize that she was there for me. I talked to her every day, without fail, while I was growing up.

I failed the first grade because I had difficulty learning to read and was tested for a special education program in kindergarten. Yet Mama believed in me and supported my dreams. In fact, we would often dream together about a future where I was a doctor. In our dream, she would have her own separate house in my backyard. In some ways, this dream helped us both escape our current situation. Daddy and other family members often told me that "people like us don't become doctors," but Mama never let me believe that my dream could not come to fruition. On the nights that she didn't work, I would lie on the living room floor while she called out homework to me repeatedly until I could recite it back to her like a well-told story. She even reviewed homework from memory with me on the days she worked during our morning ride back to Grandma's house. Mama only had a high school education but she always seemed to know about a lot of things. I came to understand that my grade improvement was not simply due to me being smart. If I worked hard, I realized, I could do well in school. Eventually I became competitive with myself and wanted to do better than I had done before.

At the beginning of the sixth grade, Daddy had agreed to let me stay with him on the nights that Mama worked. I was excited for the change to my normal routine. I enjoyed having stepsiblings with whom to play games. Daddy's wife prepared home-cooked meals. Spaghetti, enchiladas, and made-from-scratch pineapple pudding were some of my favorites. I just wanted my childhood to be a little more traditional—and I wanted more time to enjoy the four-wheelers, pool table, RV, boat, and other toys that were at Daddy's house over the years. Truth be told, I was jealous that *my* dad had provided such a seemingly wonderful life for someone else and her kids when they had their own father to do it for them.

Soon after staying with Daddy and his family didn't pan out the way that I had hoped, he dropped me off at Mama's home on Sunday after my scheduled weekend with him. Mama was there to help me get settled before she had to leave for work. She had not been gone long before Brenda called me in a panic. A neighbor, who had a police radio scanner, had called to alert her that the police were coming because I had been left home alone. Brenda told me to leave home immediately without packing any clothes and walk through the woods to Gator Hole, a secluded swimming spot not far from Mama's home, so she could pick me up there. Child protective services ultimately became involved, and after Mama explained how I had come to stay there alone while she worked, they approved the arrangement—both Brenda and my cousin, Melissa, lived nearby and could get to me rather quickly should I need them.

I never had any doubt that Daddy was behind the call to the police, and I was furious with him for it. As if it wasn't bad enough that he was charging to watch his own son and I could no longer stay with him, now it seemed he was trying to use the situation to hurt Mama. It was a good thing that my wish was only a few weeks away, and I had something to look forward to. Even though I was only eleven years old at the time, I had learned responsibility and tenacity by watching Mama.

I would do my homework in the evenings, put myself to bed, get myself up the next morning, make my breakfast, get myself together for school, and be ready to review homework with Mama when she finally made it home.

When I was alone at the house, I often called the homework hotline, which was a service provided by Louisiana Power and Light. Through the hotline, teachers volunteered their time to help kids over the phone. It was an absolutely amazing service, especially for a kid who was alone several nights a week. If I got stuck on a homework problem, help was just a phone call away. The hotline was also available to have homework checked, as long as the volunteers had a copy of the teacher's manual for the textbook. I used this service beginning in sixth grade, and I continued to do so until I graduated high school. I became a regular of sorts, known by name and able to connect with some of the same volunteers for the same subjects year after year. Sometimes, even if I knew my answers were correct, it was nice to have someone with whom to talk.

After my wish, I also frequently called Amy Albin from Starlight Children's Foundation when Mama wasn't there. I'd tell her about my day, or call to let her know when I'd done well on a test. She would also give me updates on *Growing Pains* and the wishes kids were making, and she put me on the Starlight mailing list. Even though I was home alone, I built a network of people to help encourage me and lessen Mama's worries when we were apart.

In 1989, nearly six years after Daddy left, Mama started dating

Wayne Penoli. I was afraid at first. I didn't want Mama to change as Daddy had when he'd gotten married again. Mama sensed this and took it slow; soon he would become a big part of our "village." Mama describes Wayne as a good friend, and he was. He was good to Grandma, Brenda, my nephews, and me. Mr. Wayne, as I always called him to show respect, became a part of the family through his willingness to participate in our lives in ways my dad didn't. He celebrated birthdays and holidays with us. He took family vacations with us. Later in their relationship he often stayed with me while Mama worked, lessening the amount of time I had to be alone.

I wanted Daddy to call me while I was at home just to check in to see if I was okay. Though that call never came, Wayne's did. Wayne would also accept school event invitations that had been declined by Daddy. He was often mistaken for my dad simply because he was the one who showed up, time and time again. When extra money was needed for school events or trips Wayne insisted that I give my dad the opportunity to help out, but if Daddy didn't come through, he was always more than willing to make sure that I never missed out on any opportunities. He trusted me with any new adventure I was willing to try.

We started to eat most of our meals out after Daddy left. Cooking was a chore for my overworked mother. We would order a kid's meal, I would eat what I wanted, and Mama would eat what was left. At the time, I probably thought it was one of her motherly quirks, but now I realize she was probably saving money doing what she had to do as a single mother to care for her son.

My own brief foray into cooking scrambled eggs had ended in me not cleaning the stove well enough; I came home to find potted plants covering the stove, which stayed there for years afterward. They were only removed when Mama overheard

Brenda's son Maika telling his friends that his granny kept "pot plants" on her stove.

After Wayne came into our life we began eating many of our meals at Ginny's Restaurant in Jena, sitting at the same table night after night, listening to a good mix of Dolly Parton and Kenny Rogers through the crackling speaker.

Wayne did the kinds of things a father should do. He helped me with schoolwork. He indulged me by helping me get things I thought I wanted even if Mama didn't always agree that I should have them. I remember a pair of suspenders he bought me, which I only wore once; then there was a bowl of fish I promised to take care of but never did.

His influence on me was great. But his influence on my actual dad was even greater. Wayne's presence in Mama's and my life moved Daddy to try just a little bit harder—even if he didn't realize it. This was an unexpected, welcomed outcome from my relationship with Wayne. I appreciated it as much as I appreciated Wayne's faith in me. He believed I could do whatever I wanted to do if I worked and studied hard enough. Wayne had attended college; no one from my immediate family had ever pursued higher education. And even though Wayne didn't hold any degrees I knew he could see the future doctor in me.

Mama could see my future, too. But as the vision began to take form it wasn't easy for her. I had looked forward to going away to college all summer. I had bought everything I needed for my dorm room. I was going to be roommates with Scott Cantwell, the valedictorian of the other high school in my home parish. We'd become friends through academic competitions, and his father was an emergency room physician, so his family was a source of answers and encouragement as I prepared to start working toward my dream.

I was going to college with the focus of getting into medical school, not to party or join fraternities. But I really didn't have any idea of what college actually entailed. Before college, I had spent a little time on Tech's campus. At spring testing there I received credit for algebra, trigonometry, and Spanish. I also received chemistry credit but decided to take the class anyway. I didn't want to jump in over my head. I wanted to ease into college on firm footing.

I was overcome with happiness. I was finally getting to leave Jena and everything behind. But when the day finally came for me to leave for my first year at Louisiana Tech, Mama did not want to me go. She felt my father had left and now it was my turn to walk out the door and leave her, too. She sat in the rocking chair with her arms crossed and refused to help me pack.

Why isn't she excited for me? I asked myself, lost in thought. It seemed so unlike her. *The baby with the bad heart is finally on his way to college, just as we dreamed!*

I called Brenda to share my disappointment. "Brenda, Mama is refusing to help me move. She is in her rocking chair rocking." I had started to cry at this point.

Brenda said, "She just needs a little time. She will be okay. I will come help you."

"Please do."

Brenda came to mom's house and helped load things into her minivan. Mama was still in her chair. She didn't lift a finger. I followed Brenda to Ruston in my car. Her middle son came with us. He helped unload things but made it a point to embarrass me while we were there. He was flying around campus like he was an airplane—literally making engine noises with his arms spread wide open. This day was not going exactly as I'd envisioned.

Mama arrived about twenty minutes later. When she arrived she had tears in her eyes and gave me a hug. Soon, Scott and his mom arrived, and we all set up the room together.

Now I realize that Mama was experiencing empty nest syndrome. Because of the age difference between Brenda and me, I started kindergarten in the fall of the same year Brenda had graduated high school. Mama always had only one kid in school, but she'd had a child in school for twenty-seven consecutive years, always living at home.

Finding the strength to move on is something Mama always seemed to do well. She strongly believes that God has a way of taking care of things. She often reminds me of the times she prayed over me and gave me back to God. She says there are some things we can't do on our own, and we have to have faith to carry us through.

One day, when I was just a baby, Pastor John Morgan, a nondenominational preacher from down the road, had stopped by our house unannounced to bring money for the Houston trip and my first surgery. Word had gotten to his church about the baby with the life-threatening heart problem and they wanted to help. Mama says it was probably no more than $300, but it meant so much more. Brother Morgan eventually left and moved to Winnfield, some thirty-five miles away. Mama didn't see him again until years later after Daddy had left and Brother Morgan and his wife came by for an unexpected visit.

"While in the shower this morning, the Lord laid on my heart to see how y'all were doing," he said with conviction. "I want you to know that everything is going to be all right."

Mama told him about my physical progress, and the Morgans were pleased to hear of it. But then she shared about the troubles between her and Daddy.

"The Lord will take care of it. You just need to trust Him," he reassured her.

Mama never forgot that. And since that time, she never seemed to lose faith.

But even with that faith, things were definitely not always easy. Seeing Daddy disappoint me time and time again did not sit well with her. It seemed as if he only showed up for the fun events that required no work on his part—if he showed up at all. It was unfair to her and to me.

I remember an awards banquet at Louisiana Tech University in 1997. I was being honored for my good grades and wanted to invite Daddy to the ceremony but feared he wouldn't come. To alleviate what I thought would be certain disappointment, I called the dean's office and had them send the invitation directly to him. I figured if he came, great. If not, I had no way to know for sure if he ever got the invite.

In the end he came, but Mama got upset. Not only was there the possibility that I might be hurt again by his not showing up, there I was, arranging things for his convenience, trying in advance to soften my disappointment when he failed me. Even when he did arrive, I was so happy that Mama was disturbed. I would bend over backward to spend every moment with him. It seemed to Mama that he was only there to pull me away from her.

Sometimes God also uses us to care for each other. Like the pastor who delivered the money and imparted his wisdom on our doorstep all those years ago, Mama has been motivated by God to be that someone who cares for me. Dream or no dream, I would not be anything without her.

CHAPTER SEVEN

WITH A LITTLE HELP FROM MY FRIENDS

It was cool enough I got to visit the set of *Growing Pains* in 1989, thanks to Starlight Children's Foundation. The icing on the cake was that I was going to be able to watch the finished product, back at home in rural Louisiana.

My grandma came to stay with me the night it aired. Mama was working, of course. It was October 18, the very night all eyes, including ours, should have been glued to the 1989 World Series. The previous night's game was being played at Candlestick Park in San Francisco until about 5:04 p.m., West Coast time, when an earthquake rocked the city on the hill.

The World Series was disrupted as approximately 62,000 people experienced the jolt. Instantly, it became the first major earthquake in the United States broadcast live on national television. The World Series didn't resume play until October 27. When the lights at Candlestick went out Grandma and I looked at each other across the couch, startled. And then a familiar theme song came on. ABC had decided to show the episode of *Growing Pains* that I had seen taped out in Burbank.

And there it was!

The trip to California had been like an earthquake for me—a big jolt that rocked my world. I was struggling to overcome the feeling that I'd spend the majority of my time sitting on the sidelines of life. A small town like Jena can be made to feel even smaller when you can't do what others are doing.

I bore the surgical and emotional scars to show for a childhood plagued with things gone wrong. My first surgery, at the age of two, was followed by a hernia operation and further cardiac procedures. I'd had my last heart cath right before I was to start the sixth grade and just before I received my wish. Mama and Daddy always seemed to be at odds with one another about something—usually me.

Meeting Jeremy Miller could not have come at a better time. Have you ever been so low you felt like you would never get up again? Starlight Children's Foundation was a great pick-me-up when I felt like that. After all the excitement of having my wish granted, the prospect of returning home to deal with things in my life was exciting in its own way. My wish changed me from the inside out and set me on a new path. I had a new way of looking at life. Even if I couldn't do everything everyone else was doing, I could still do some pretty cool stuff.

I started to believe that I could really become a doctor and make something out of the gifts and talents God had given me. The key was in believing it all started with my life, however imperfect or uncommon it was. The wish opened my eyes to that and to all the things that God had provided for me.

One of the most important of these was friends. I am not saying I had a lot. When I was young, my life mostly revolved around my family. While Brenda always seemed to have lots of friends around, I could count my good companions on less than one hand. But they made up for it in quality.

***

Jarred Pugh, my oldest friend, was number one. We were from the same rural community. We started our lives on the same road, living just a couple of miles from each other, in the countryside near Jena. Our fathers both worked in the oil field, and we'd met before we even started kindergarten. Some years later, his mother, whom I knew very well by then, taught me sophomore English in high school. She had done the same for Brenda some fourteen years earlier. And as a teenager Brenda sometimes babysat Jarred and his sisters. It was no surprise that Jarred and I became friends; our lives were pretty much intertwined.

The Pugh home was one of the few places I was allowed to spend the night while growing up. In like fashion, Jarred would sometimes have sleepovers with me on nights I stayed with Daddy. We remained good friends even though circumstances seemed to conspire to pull us apart. Jarred and I moved from kindergarten to Mrs. Poole's first-grade class together. But by the end of the school year, I was held back while he graduated to the next grade. I had been labeled slow, and my teachers encouraged Mama to have me tested for special education classes. She would have none of it; according to her, the trouble came from having to deal with a lot of emotional stuff brought on by my dad. After all, I was the product of a broken home and the trauma it produces.

When she was told I would have to repeat first grade because of low grades and slow reading habits, Mama complied. But that didn't stop her from taking me to a different school in Grant

Parish before I started my second go-around of first grade. It was a wise decision, because it prevented me from being labeled negatively for the rest of my academic career.

I flourished at my new school, making mostly A's and B's. Even though I remained in one of the slower-reading groups, by the fourth grade, I was placed in one of the top math groups. But it was far from an ideal situation. I soon made a new friend, Ricky Martin (no—not the *loca*-living pop star you're thinking of)—but he couldn't come to my home to play on the weekends, because no one was to know that I actually lived in the neighboring parish of LaSalle. The move also started the car trips back and forth to my grandma's house so that I could catch the bus and Mama could make it to work on time. And, of course, it meant there was no way I could continue attending school with Jarred. We both played Little League for a couple of years when my dad and his wife coached, but Jarred and I were never on the same team.

The fact that our families knew each other and that Jarred occasionally spent weekends at my dad's house during our middle school and junior high years was the saving grace that helped us remain friends. As we grew older, we spent most of our time together playing video games, hanging out in the woods doing kid stuff, and just talking sports.

Jarred remembers being at my dad's house more often than I came to his. He still has a fond memory of me riding my four-wheel ATV through the woods to his front door. He couldn't believe that I had made the four-mile trip. I explained excitedly that I had known I could do it, because I had thought through the plan. The woods were the best route. Heading down the road would have been a rugged ten-mile ride on the off-road vehicle. Plowing through trees and underbrush, whipping down dirt roads, I soon emerged onto his front lawn, dirty and victorious.

Jarred says he always knew I was different. Kids have a way of sensing things like that. But it wasn't my heart that had brought him to that conclusion. He didn't know how sick I was until high school. It was the other things that defined me. I didn't play sports—at least not like he did. By the time we reached middle and high school, Jarred was involved in all kinds of athletics. He was a self-described "jock nerd"—a quarterback who liked computers, history, and physics. I liked those things, as well. I also admired the fact that Jarred was in the gifted and talented program at school. He admired the fact that I'd taught myself to type.

After playing two years of Little League baseball, I found that I was more comfortable in the press box keeping the official scorebook, operating the scoreboard, and announcing the game. In fact, this was my first paid job. I made seven dollars a game and worked at the baseball park from seventh grade through high school.

I met Jarred's gifted teacher, Ms. Bridget Thomsen, while volunteering in the park's concession stand during a charity tournament. She called Mama and encouraged her to have me tested. When I passed and entered the program in my freshman year of high school, it gave Jarred and me the opportunity to redefine our friendship into something it had never been before. We took a few accelerated classes together and participated in some of the same clubs—Beta Club, Future Business Leaders of America, Quiz Bowl, and student council. We would often travel to compete in academic competitions throughout the state on weekends. In 1995, he and I both earned spots to represent Louisiana at the national Future Business Leaders of America competition in Orlando, Florida. I had placed first in the state in Information Processing (still never having learned how to type the "correct" way), while he had placed first in Mr. Future Business Leader of

America. And that's what rekindled and solidified our relation-ship—an unspoken friendly rivalry when it came to academics.

Based on all the time we spent together with some occa-sional breaks in between, I've always thought of Jarred as being extremely bright, well spoken, very charismatic, and someone who could be trusted. Jarred had seen my scar during sleepovers, so he knew about my heart. When I returned from *Growing Pains*, I shared with him my hope that I would one day be a pedi-atric cardiologist. And unlike some members of my family, who denied even the possibility of something like that happening for me, Jarred believed in me from the moment I said it.

He was the perfect accomplice in helping me achieve my goal. Jarred made it easy for me to concentrate on my studies, especially in high school. It wasn't an oddity to him that I was so intently focused on academics. He never labeled me crazy, even when Ms. Thomsen became very ill during my first year of high school and in her absence I read the Algebra I and II books and taught myself. Sure, I would ask older students or math teachers at school for help when I got stuck on a problem, but I learned. As a result, I was able to skip geometry and go straight into trig-onometry my junior year. I had a near-perfect score on the math part of the American College Test, or ACT as it is commonly known, and I ultimately placed in the top ten in the state Beta Club mathematics competition my senior year.

Luckily, I came to realize that my trouble with words was limited to reading. My seventh-grade teacher had helped me to understand that the rules of sentence structure, grammar, and punctuation were very methodical. Once she explained it this way, something clicked; I began to think of writing as another form of math. I threw myself into studying grammatical forms and exceptions. Though I still had trouble with reading, I was the only student in my high school class to receive a perfect score on the state's standardized writing exam required for graduation.

"Stop throwing the curve in our classes! You need to slow down and take up a time-consuming hobby!" Maggie Ashley wrote in my freshman yearbook.

I could have slowed down (and no doubt some of my classmates wanted me to), but I had set out to get something that was made attainable to me by a wish. Jarred, the high school quarterback, made sure I was never bullied because of it. He was always there to support my dreams. Jarred and I kept in touch after high school, and he even came to my graduation from Louisiana Tech. He cried when I walked across the stage to receive my diploma; he was one of a few people who knew the path I had taken to reach this milestone.

***

Matt Ganey was another God-given friend. I met him at Fellowship Baptist Church. We were in the same youth group and went on church trips together. Matt is two years older than I am; while I was attending Fellowship Elementary, he was at Jena High School playing football. What connected me to Matt first were all the church activities; I was invited to a few game nights at his home as I was growing up.

We grew closer as I got into high school. A couple of times we drove to Alexandria, Louisiana, some forty-five miles away, to take the ACT. Like me, Matt wanted to be a doctor. He just wasn't quite set on his specialty. Because he was older than me, he was in the enviable position of leaving for college first.

When the time came for me to pursue higher education and begin my journey toward becoming a pediatric cardiologist, Matt was already a junior at Louisiana Tech University, studying in the preprofessional sciences program. He lived in the honors dorm and invited me to come up and stay with him on Super Bowl Sunday in 1996. The next day I went to class with him.

I had been looking at Baylor University in Waco, Texas, although this fell out of favor when Dr. Vargo told me that the university was not associated with Baylor College of Medicine. Emory University in Atlanta was another consideration. But after my visit to Louisiana Tech, I was convinced that was where I wanted to go. It was a smaller campus, with a nice feeling of community, and I liked the students and professors I had met through Matt.

But Matt really was the reason I even considered going to Tech in the first place. He knew that my ability to pay for college was a huge concern; I had put aside birthday money throughout my childhood, and Mama had made a contribution to my college savings account with each paycheck she earned, but we had only saved about $3,000, barely enough to cover my first quarter. Matt reassured me that I had every reason to believe I would receive a full scholarship, and he was right.

There were a few others from Jena at Tech, and it was like a ready-made group of friends. Because we were from the same hometown, Matt was committed to having my back and watching out for me in the same way Jarred had in high school. It was something he was willing to do for anyone who was from Central Louisiana, both in college and dental school, which is where he eventually wound up.

I always liked being around Matt. He and his family made me feel included. His mom never failed to talk to me whenever she saw me at school, and when I moved schools, she was a familiar face. Because of his determination to reach out, he and I grew closer at college than we had ever been at home. The first year of college is a maneuvering act—one in which Matt helped me out.

"Which professors should I take?" "Who should I avoid?" I'd ask, trying to find classes where outside reading was minimal. Being a slow reader was something I'd learned to deal with, and I refused to allow it to stop me. It just took some careful planning on my part. Most of the time I just opted to take math-based electives. In my free time, when I wasn't studying, I played Frisbee with Matt and his friends. My physical activities were limited, but my friend Matt never left me out. He'd never assume I couldn't do anything, nor would he pressure me. He'd simply leave the choice up to me.

If you ask Matt what I was like as a kid growing up at home and in college, he'll say that most people thought I was smart, shy, and unapproachable. But he saw my "unapproachability" differently. He found it easy to relate to me, especially if he was talking about something that interested me. Matt believes that some people just felt out of my league whenever they were around me; I was too quick for them. I was too quick for him, too. He remembers studying things for hours that he said came so easily to me. But what I was surprised at was how easily his friendship came and how much support it provided me.

***

I left California after receiving my wish, hoping to find a way to stay in touch with my new friend Jeremy Miller. I didn't want to lose contact with him or the feelings that had inspired me to move forward. The two of us began writing to each other for a while, and that lasted until the show left the air, around the time I was in eighth grade. We lost touch at that point. It was prehistoric. In 1992, Facebook was just something that happened when you fell asleep reading a good novel.

That same year, on the last day of eighth grade, I met Cindy Corley. I had been invited to the end-of-year party for the high school gifted program so I could meet other gifted students before starting the program in the fall. Cindy was there with her mom, picking up her brother. She was a year younger than me and just finishing the seventh grade. We would be going to different schools when the school year started, but Cindy's mom would become my physical science teacher during my freshman year and my chemistry teacher during my junior year. She would eventually become one of my favorite teachers, because she believed in my ability to achieve my dream from the moment I first entered high school; she had, in fact, given me lots of useful information and a tour of the school before I began, and then she recruited me to help give tours to other incoming students.

The first time Cindy and I spent any amount of time together, we were working the overnight shift in the concession stand at a marathon softball game to raise money for the Muscular Dystrophy Association. We enjoyed an instant connection, passing the time by singing songs like "Hot Child in the City" along with the radio while making soft drinks for our customers. Little did she know that it was the closest thing I had to a theme song. But there was time to learn stuff like that, because this was just the start of a very special relationship.

In the beginning Cindy didn't really know much about my family other than that my parents had divorced and I lived the majority of the time with Mama. It took a while for me to share more. Over our teenage years, I eventually revealed my entire story. I told her about my struggles with my dad's emotional and physical absence and that I always longed for a family like the one on *Growing Pains*. Cindy noticed I was often alone and that there were certain feelings I held onto regarding my parents' divorce. She saw that I still blamed myself (and my illness) for my parents' separation. Cindy reminded me that I had no part in their unhappiness with each other. To the degree to which I could embrace this, I did. I thanked God for bringing someone like Cindy into my life; she made it so easy for me to be transparent.

She came along at a very serious time in my life. Based on all I knew about my condition, I believed I wouldn't be around much longer. In the back of my mind, I still thought I wouldn't make it past the age of twenty. But even though I never thought I would live long enough to be a practicing physician, I wanted to be remembered for trying to reach my goal. It's no exaggeration to say there was a sense of urgency.

As a friend, Cindy gave me space to be goal-oriented and self-driven, while allowing for my moments of quietness and thoughtfulness. She says I have always been a supportive friend, but in truth, I always felt I'd learned that because of her. She knew a great deal about my medical issues, more as an adult than as an adolescent, but she never let it color her interactions with me. Cindy didn't define me by the condition of my health. When I first told her about my heart, I simply said I had a heart problem that had been repaired with surgery when I was a baby; I wanted her to know that I believed I could do everything that other people our age could do. Even after she learned more, it never changed how she treated me.

I graduated high school a year earlier than Cindy. We ended up going to different colleges, but in accordance with my life and every real relationship I ever had, we did not lose touch. We found ways to share great memories, like the time Cindy attended the Cadaver Ball with me in New Orleans during my second year of medical school. Yes, that is what this medical school tradition is really called. The name "cadaver" is used because it celebrates the end of gross anatomy for first-year students. (I guess in med school you have to take fun where you can find it, even if it sounds a little creepy.)

That year the ball was held at the children's museum, and we had the best time exploring the exhibits. There was a pulley system where you could lift yourself up, adding pulleys to reduce the weight. There were simple machines to play with, and a pretend store where you had to serve as your own cashier. We mingled with my classmates, enjoying the novelty of being dressed up while playing children's games, continuing to talk and laugh as the party spilled out of the museum and into the French Quarter. What a party—I felt like a kid! That's the best part of my relationship with her. We have always found ways to live in the moment and have fun no matter where we find ourselves.

Even as adults, when we traveled together, we did it like kids. On a recent cruise, Cindy's son, Jamey, had brought his favorite stuffed animal, an alien named Mama Green, along. While the cruise ship staff was entertaining him we took his camera and Mama Green all over the ship and took pictures of it in different locations. We had a blast. The look on Jamey's face when he reviewed the pictures on his camera (and discovered all the adventures his stuffed animal had gotten up to) was priceless.

Maybe she was so understanding because we'd both faced medical conditions in our youth. Cindy suffered from Crohn's disease, a chronic inflammatory bowel disease, throughout high school, and she was away from school for extended periods of time. Because of this, we just "got" each other. We would make the same nerdy science jokes and complete each other's sentences.

Cindy and I also dated off and on through the years. The

biggest obstacle to our relationship has always been timing. While in high school, I drove my ATV through the woods to her home a few times, just hoping that she would be outside so I could confess my feelings, but she never was. Just as I completed my first year of college, my sister's youngest son had a doctor's appointment at the children's hospital in New Orleans. I agreed to go even though it was the day of Jena High School's graduation, and I knew I would miss seeing my friends in the class behind mine walk across the stage to receive their diplomas. But I also knew Cindy was hospitalized at the same hospital, and I wanted to see her. She never knew I had made the trip to New Orleans to check on her because her doctor had released her just in time for her to make it back to Jena for graduation. I was at least able to catch her salutatorian address on Jena's radio station during the drive home.

While I was at Louisiana Tech, we rarely saw each other, but we kept in contact by email. She and I reconnected only after I started medical school. I began rotations in my third year, two-month blocks working in hospitals in several different areas (family medicine, surgery, pediatrics, and more). As Cindy was working at one of the hospitals near Jena as a pediatric nurse, I often chose to do away rotations at hospitals closer to Jena so I could be closer to her.

After I left Louisiana for my residency and fellowship, Cindy and I lost contact again. She got married, becoming Cindy Corley Sanders, and had a child. After her husband died in a car accident, we began to talk again. She came to my office's Christmas party during my first year of employment in Texas as an attending physician, and attended the Fiesta de Los Niños fundraiser to support Driscoll Children's Hospital with me in Corpus Christi. At one point I also brought her out to Los Angeles to accompany me to a Starlight Children's Foundation charity event. We spent the following day at Disneyland, "testing the rides so we could make recommendations for the pediatric patients." It brought me back to my wish in 1989 all over again.

Over the years, Cindy has made several handmade gifts for me. She's artistic that way and quite talented. One such gift was a cross-stitched doctor bear. A few years after I had hung it on my wall, I noticed the backing had come apart. When I took it down, I found a letter she had written addressed to me, letting me know that she would always care for me.

I feel a special bond with Cindy's son, Jamey. In some ways, we are a lot alike. I think Jamey has helped Cindy understand me better, and I hoped I could play a similar role for him as the one Mama's friend, Wayne, had played for me.

Cindy and I were not able to make our relationship work in the long run—long-distance relationships can be complicated and difficult, and our lives have simply taken us in different directions. However, I have always appreciated her friendship and the support she's given me, and I am incredibly thankful for the role that she and her son played in my life.

As an adolescent, I tried to fit in where I could. And when I couldn't, I threw myself into my academics. It was my way of escaping because it allowed me to dream of a different life. My goal was to never be treated differently, even though I *was* different. God gave me friends like Jarred, Matt, and Cindy to encourage me along the way.

CHAPTER EIGHT

THE RIGHT PERSON FOR THE RIGHT SEASON

I remember lying in bed with tears in my eyes before high school graduation. My desire to attend college was so strong I could hardly fathom the fact that it was finally going to happen. So much of my struggle had culminated in this moment of reflection. I was particularly mindful of the days leading up to receiving my diploma. Of course, that was the week Daddy chose to have papers served on Mama over a thirteen-year-old property settlement.

It didn't seem to matter to him that what I had worked so hard for was about to happen. He had himself to focus on. In my disappointment I decided to revise my valedictory address. As planned, I chose to thank each family member for their contribution to my academic success, but I debated on leaving Daddy out altogether. In the end, I decided to thank him, too. I recognized him for his "steady support." These two words referenced his court-dictated, monthly child-support payments. I knew Daddy got the message as to how I felt. In the same way, he eventually got a similar message through an announcement that appeared in *The Jena Times* leading up to my departure.

Like many small-town newspapers, *The Jena Times* ran local stories that would never make it into a big-city paper. At the time, I didn't realize how unique it was to have every award and honor announced to the local community. Jena is close knit, and many people seemed genuinely proud of my accomplishments and would offer their congratulations when I was in town. Once I started receiving college scholarships, they were announced in the weekly publication. For one of them, I identified myself as the son of Carolyn Phillips, leaving out any mention of my dad. Whenever someone would ask about the newspaper's mistake in omitting him, I would tell them "no mistake was made" and then honestly explain what was going on in my family.

Jena is a small place, and it didn't take long before Daddy called me, very upset.

"Why are you telling everyone about my business with your mom? You are ruining my reputation."

"I'm sorry if you don't like what I've told. But I haven't said anything that isn't true."

"I didn't want to displace you from the family home when you were in school, which is why I waited until now," he insisted.

"Your monthly child-support payments haven't changed since you divorced Mama, even though you've gotten several promotions and raises over the years."

He tried to object, but I continued. "I'm only telling people the truth. If you don't like it, it's on you to change. *Do* better and you'll *be* better. My life will go on, with or without you—just as it has since you left on my fifth birthday."

I wanted Daddy to know he could choose to be a part of my future or not; the choice was his to make. But he would not disrupt my life and my goals any longer. I told him that if he did, I would simply forget him and tell my children he died a long time ago. He grew quiet immediately, and I knew my words had cut him to the bone.

But that's the point at which I was. I was moving on, and not just to college. I was closing the door on that part of my life and had no desire to carry old baggage with me. I didn't want to lose my father. But I had already mourned the loss of his presence for a very long time. This was one of the few times that I expressed how I actually felt in such a clear and audible way that he seemed to comprehend it. Some of the choices he'd made had affected me profoundly. Maybe the magnitude of what he'd done finally hit home. After a tense silence, Daddy surprised me by offering to take me to college and buy my books for my first quarter.

That quarter I was scheduled to take calculus. While we were at the register paying for everything, Daddy asked, "What's cal-cool-us?" That made me smile, mostly because we were spending time together, one on one. And that was all I really ever wanted from him. He seemed softer, more interested in what I was doing than he had been before. He told me later that it was on that day he realized I'd likely never return to Jena.

Even though Daddy never finished high school, I was always fascinated by how he used math on the job. He'd begun his career doing the dirtiest jobs on the oil rig but had moved up to the position of "company man," helping to organize the contract services required to drill an oil well. He did daily calculations on his adding machine. Perhaps I actually got some of my mathematical prowess from him.

Daddy got me a Texas Instruments Speak & Math for a birthday gift. He even got me an adding machine with the paper roll like the one in his office. Much of my childhood play revolved around numbers—I could go for hours crunching numbers. When I was in second grade, I wanted to know how my teachers calculated my grades, so Mama showed me how to average numbers on the calculator. It was pure entertainment for me.

Years later in college, while in Dr. Zotov's calculus class, seated next to me in the front row, I met a student named Matt LeBlanc—yet another friend in my life who shares a name with someone famous.

God seemed to put Matt in my life for a purpose. We always chatted in the minutes before class would start. He was from Dallas, Texas, and majoring in civil engineering. His original plan was to be a cadet at the Air Force Academy in Colorado Springs, but that didn't work out, so he chose to follow in his father's footsteps and enroll in the Air Force ROTC program at Tech. On a few occasions when I was young, Mama told me that my heart condition would keep me from being drafted into service, so I'd never thought much about the military or why people would be drawn to serve. I'd just assumed it was a good thing; my uncles had served in the navy, and Mama seemed relieved I wouldn't have an opportunity to do the same. Matt changed my perception of those who serve in the military. I have nothing but respect and admiration for those who serve.

Matt and I struck up a friendship after the professor handed back our first exam. Matt likes to say that our grades were comparable on that first test. What I remember—a bit more clearly—is that I had beaten his high score and gotten 101 percent, making him snatch my exam paper off my desk and say, "Let me see that!" How I had managed to earn such a score on an exam with no advertised bonus remains a mystery. We began to do our homework independently and then review it together, a friendly rivalry that solidified our friendship.

I had grown up around smart people, but having come from Jena High School, I worried about being underprepared for college compared to those who had come from more academically rigorous high schools. Matt made me realize that I could compete and that I wasn't alone in my enjoyment in the subtleties of higher math. He would crack jokes about the complex concepts, the two of us laughing as we left the classroom.

We finished Calculus I, and then we ended up taking our next three calculus classes together, as well. Our eventual claim to fame came when we were the only two students in our Calculus II class to be exempted from taking the final. Our professor, Dr. Thrasher, shocked everyone, including Matt and me, when he wrote our names on the board before excusing us from the room.

Matt asked me to attend the Christian Student Center meetings with him at the Ruston Church of Christ. The church had a college group that met on Tuesday nights. One day, while at a church cookout, some of the guys decided to play flag football. Without thinking, Matt threw the football to me before heading out. Instead of me catching it, it hit my chest and bounced off. I felt more embarrassment than physical pain. I was painfully shy when around new people, and Matt's pass upset me because it made me feel out of my element and completely put on the spot. I had never played sports in high school.

Matt called me on the phone later that afternoon. I think he sensed he had upset me with his football throw, though he didn't understand why. When I explained it to him, Matt told me I was needed on the church intramural team. He said without me they would not have enough guys to make a team. I reluctantly agreed to let him sign me up, incredibly nervous. I didn't even know how to play! Matt had to teach me the game of football, including how to throw and catch the ball.

Matt became good at finding "new" experiences for me. He realized I'd been exposed to few of the physical and sports experiences so many young boys get to share. Once when it was raining, he called and told me to put on old clothes and meet him at his dorm. We went out to one of the fields on campus, where we ran and slid in the mud, face first. It was so much fun; I'm sure those watching from the sidelines thought we were crazy, but I didn't care. We had become good friends, and I was comfortable trying new adventures with him. (I did, however, throw my clothes away to avoid explaining the filthy mess to my mother when she did the laundry.)

I told Matt at first only that I had a heart problem. He discovered more when I was required to wear a monitor for a day and do some aerobic exercises. I chose to jog. Dr. Vargo thought it was a good idea, as long as I had someone with me on the off chance something happened. I needed someone who would know to get help. I asked Matt to be that someone.

Looking back, I didn't realize the risks as I do now. The possibility that my heart could beat abnormally and lead to sudden death due to exercise did not register, and I did not take serious precautions. Now, when I go to the gym I ensure that a trainer is present and that they know about my condition and where the defibrillator is located in the event of an emergency. Back then, I figured Dr. Vargo was just worried about me being too winded.

But life for a heart-defect patient is full of risks, and the benefits of exercise—both physical and emotional—can outweigh the small chance of something going wrong. The jog went well, and best of all, I felt more "normal." After the testing had been done, Dr. Vargo encouraged me to keep exercising. So Matt and I continued jogging. Actually, it was more like a fast walk most of the time; I never could run more than half a mile without tiring. But I felt myself improving slowly. Before long, we moved on to lifting weights and tried other team sports.

I benefited so much from exercising with Matt at Tech that I continued working out in med school and during my fellowship at Mayo Clinic. Today, I still try to squeeze in some form of exercise whenever possible—one of my friends recently taught me to play racquetball.

***

Back at Tech, Matt and I tried to make a point of attending church for Sunday service, Wednesday Bible study, and the college group on Tuesday nights. I was pretty consistent when it came to going to services at the Christian Student Center. Dr. Kathleen Johnston, who taught my sophomore calculus-based physics class for engineering students, still remembers the time I decided to go to an event happening at the church the night before my very first physics test, before she even knew me by name. I got up to leave her study session early, hoping to sneak out the back. Her voice rang out loudly, asking where I was going.

Dr. Johnston had a reputation for being tough; in fact, on the first day of class, she told us that only about half of the students who started the class would complete it. When I told her where I was going, she said, "Boy, praying isn't going to help you pass."

Imagine her surprise when I got a perfect score.

When Dr. Johnston passed back the graded tests, she held mine until the end and made a statement to the whole class that one student had an unprecedented score on the first exam. When I stepped forward to claim my exam, she immediately recognized me as the student who had left early to go to church. She chuckled. "Well, well, well. It seems prayer does indeed work—even in physics class."

After that, Dr. Johnston became my mentor. I greatly admired her teaching, and she was one of my most influential professors at Louisiana Tech. Her class stands out as one of my favorites. Her tests were unusual. Unlike the questions in my textbook, which used numbers and resulted in a final numerical answer, she used only variables. I would have to think outside the box, drawing on my knowledge of math theory, making educated guesses based on my training, and linking different concepts. She taught me to think critically and apply the knowledge I had learned in other disciplines to find solutions.

I hadn't told many of my professors about my condition; I wanted to be known for the work I did, not for my heart. I was able to distinguish myself in Dr. Johnston's class in a different way, however. Unlike many of the other premed students, who were interested in finding the correct answer and scoring high, I really wanted to understand the material in depth, and Dr. Johnston and I bonded over this interest.

Another one of my favorite professors was Dr. Ramu Ramachandran, who is endearingly referred to as "Dr. Ramu" by his colleagues and students. He was the program chair for chemistry, and he taught me two quarters of physical chemistry. I was impressed when I realized he was one of the authors of the solutions manual that accompanied the textbook. It was the first time I had been taught a course by someone who had helped write the book.

After graduation, Dr. Ramu managed to keep up with me through Facebook. He nominated me for chemistry's Distinguished Alumnus Award from the College of Engineering and Science in 2014 because he felt that I had accomplished a lot professionally at a young age. Perhaps he was right. At the award banquet I realized that many of the other recipients of the award from other disciplines had graduated from Tech before I had even been born.

When I was a student at Louisiana Tech I never expected to return to campus to receive such an honor. As my twentieth birthday approached, during my sophomore year, my heart was burdened with questions about my own mortality. I wasn't afraid of dying. After all, ten out of ten people die. I had long accepted this as my eventual fate. But I was afraid of not leaving a mark, of not being remembered. I had spent my life seeking out opportunities to give back and give my life purpose. But the idea of dying before I could achieve my dream weighed heavily on my mind.

I knew I had made mistakes throughout my life, and I wanted to make sure my heart was right with God. I followed the steps of salvation, and I could not have asked for a more loving and supportive church family than I found in the people who met to worship at the Ruston Church of Christ. Church brought me a sense of peace, even over the bigger questions.

Though we came from different backgrounds, on some level, Matt could relate to where I grew up. His parents were from DeQuincy, Louisiana, a small town much like Jena. Matt was realistic and positive when I described my situation. When I opened up and shared about my fears regarding my heart condition and my disappointment in Daddy, Matt would always reply with a focus on the positive: "Look how well your mom did. She made sure you'd make more out of your life. She helped you rise above your circumstances. You're very lucky to have her."

When I entered college, I started out as a biomedical engineering major. Early in my sophomore year, I switched to chemistry. I lived in the honors dorm. I made friends. We were a pretty tight community as far as college dorms go. But for the most part, my life at college consisted of getting up early for class, studying in the afternoon, and going to bed earlier than the other people in my dorm. As pedestrian as that may seem, my life really did open up when I got to college. I met different kinds of people at school and church. I even became friends with Matt's future wife, Tiffany, before the two of them started dating.

Matt started dating Tiffany during our sophomore year. It was around the same time I started dealing with depression and uncertainty about my future.

I'll admit I was perplexed about their relationship at first. Growing up, Mama made it clear that she felt romantic involvement should wait until academic pursuits are complete; I think she was afraid that I would allow someone to get in the way of my achieving my dream. I tended to agree. My solitary childhood and family chaos certainly affected my views on relationships, but that wasn't the real reason I was so independent. I realized early on that life is short. I am not comfortable with the idea of having to compromise for another, and it's important to me to be able to make decisions and accomplish my goals independently. There is much to do; my focus has always centered on living my life exactly the way I want to live it.

When Matt and Tiffany began to date, I did see his focus change a bit, which seemed to support Mama's point. Marriage was nowhere on my radar, and I had a hard time understanding why Matt would want to get married so young, before graduating. But then again, Matt's parents were still together and very much in love; he had grown up with an entirely different perception of marriage than I did.

***

While I was away at college, Mama continued to be a strong influence on my life. Most of the time it was welcome. Throughout college, she took me on a series of road trips along with Wayne, Aunt Deana, and Grandma. She helped me learn about history and literature by bringing me to historical sights and locations, filling me in on facts that would resonate and stick in my brain. We'd go several thousand miles in one direction, return home, and then head out on the road in a different direction, based on our whims or what I was learning in my history classes. We drove up the Pacific Coast Highway, starting from San Diego, to see where Wayne had grown up, help him reconnect with his sister, and visit sites from my lessons on the Donner Party and *Grapes of Wrath*. We saw Crater Lake, visited a Pennsylvania amusement park, and drove through New York and Vermont. Mama would save all year for these trips and work hard to make history come to life for me.

But every now and then her influence became too strong, and I needed to step up and say something. For example, after our monthlong summer road trip through Vermont, New York, and Pennsylvania, we got back to town with only a day or two before I had to get back to school for the start of my sophomore year. I decided to visit Daddy for a few hours. Mama got upset.

"Here I am washing my guts out, and you go see *him!*" Mama cried, referring to how much laundry she had to do before school began. During the previous year, she would pick up my dirty clothes, wash them, and then bring them back to school neatly hung in plastic bags—my personal dry cleaning service.

I was incredibly grateful for how much she had pampered me. I also knew she wasn't really complaining about washing clothes. After all, she seemed to *enjoy* doing that for me. She was upset because my time had to be divided between her and Daddy. It had been that way since the divorce. If the family had remained intact, they could have spent time with me *together*, so neither lost out. But now she felt like she was losing out whenever I was away. The school year was approaching, and she just wanted to spend as much time with me as possible. I told her not to worry about my laundry anymore. I would figure it out when I got to college.

In the end, I recruited Matt's help to show me how to wash my own clothes, and I did my laundry all that year, even though she offered many times to resume her weekly laundry service. When I returned home for summer break the next year, Mama started to wash my clothes again. But when she started to only wash a single pair of blue jeans, I quickly told her, "All of my clothes have met, mixed, and mingled in the washer, and they all seem to get along just fine. You might as well wash a whole load."

Mama and I were finally over "laundry-gate." She gave in and stopped washing my clothes one item at a time. To this day, I still think it was a stand worth taking. It's part of growing up and becoming a man—knowing what is right for yourself and for your own life.

Matt may have felt I depended a lot on him during my first two years in college. Perhaps that was true. During the summer, I often saved my money to visit him and his family in Texas. It was a pretty big deal to fly from my little town to Dallas for the weekend, but his family had become a second family to me. They were my real-life "Seaver family." Every day felt like a sitcom with them; we would attend church and then all go out to lunch together, play board games, or take trips to the lake. Friends were always welcome, and Matt and his sister Aimee would tease each other playfully. The mood was light and full of laughter. The first time I met Matt's dad, he was sitting at the kitchen table wearing Homer Simpson boxers; we all still burst out laughing every time it is brought up.

I learned a lot about Matt from the stories he told around his family's dinner table. They would chatter on about anything and everything, all completely themselves. I told a story one time, snorting with laughter, about how Matt's computer floppy disk had stopped working. He threw it, stomped on it, and then rubbed it against the wall like a crazy person. Unsurprisingly, it had not worked. His mother, laughing, piped in with a story about the time a cassette his father was playing got jammed. His dad had thrown the cassette reel across the yard, walked over, picked it up, then threw it back in the other direction.

Once in the cafeteria Matt asked if I thought he could fit a whole muffin in his mouth. The next thing I knew, he had stuffed it in there and was chewing muffin for about five minutes. He was very proud of his accomplishment.

In college Matt had a fast sports car, and I asked him to show me what his car could do. We sped through town at nearly a hundred miles an hour. A decade later I lived in South Texas. I went up to Austin to help him and his dad put a swing set together for one of his kids. Matt had made some changes to his new car. He and his dad decided to take it for a drive and invited me to come along. Matt's dad drove, and I found myself going at what felt like warp speed again. Matt's dad was a pilot, and he just said that he was used to driving faster than that with his feet on the runway. All I could envision was the newspaper headline: *Pilot, Engineer, and Physician Go to Jail for Speeding!*

I often think that the people you meet in this life are there for a purpose. Sometimes that purpose is for you; sometimes it is for them. And at times, you both seem to benefit, even if the reciprocity of the friendship may not be immediately apparent. And these reciprocal friendships are one of life's most special blessings.

When I first met Matt, I was always worried we'd lose contact after college. I clearly had a residual fear of abandonment—and I've always wanted to believe that my close friends would remain a part of my life forever, in one way or another. As my time in Ruston was coming to an end, the fear became more and more real. I graduated Louisiana Tech in four years. Matt completed his degree a little later, and he would eventually earn a PhD in civil engineering from the University of Texas.

Matt married Tiffany before our senior year in 1999. I was an usher at their wedding. Since that time, after all these years, I've witnessed him become a very loving husband and father. He's been in the military for more than fifteen years now, becoming a lieutenant colonel in the United States Air Force, where he currently works as a civil engineer. Even though he didn't get to attend the Air Force Academy as a cadet, he did end up teaching cadets. Sometimes the things we desire in this life come in God's timing, not ours.

I have experienced this time and again. I am thankful Matt attended Louisiana Tech because he was the friend I needed during that season of my life. When I left the school, Matt reassured me that we would be lifelong friends. I'm glad to say he remains a man true to his word.

Matt and I remained friends because of all we share. We love learning, we have high values, and we share a strong faith. Where we differ is in our physicality and, at times, our social acumen. I would let nothing stand in the way of my goals, even if it impacted my social life. But that never mattered to him.

Matt knows I spent a great part of my college life thinking

about dying young, and so other concerns often took a backseat. But what he may not know, until reading these words, is that it was friendship like ours that kept me moving forward into the unknown.

CHAPTER NINE

MY WELL-KEPT SECRET

E ven though my first year of college had been successful I had a well-kept secret that made me doubt my potential. Word had gotten out among my high school classmates that I had a very good score on the ACT, but none of them knew I actually took the ACT six times and only released my best score. While my score on the math part was consistently in the top 1 percent nationally, my reading scores were all over the map. In fact, the first time I took the exam, I received a reading score in the bottom fourth of all the students.

I had discovered that I learned best by hearing. Throughout grade school and high school, Mama read my class notes aloud until I could recite them back to her like a well-told story. At Louisiana Tech, I compensated for her absence by typing my notes immediately after class and reading them aloud repeatedly. I took math-based classes for my electives because they took considerably less effort. I also researched the professors to find the classes with minimal assigned outside reading.

While my difficulty with reading certainly made me doubt

myself, it also made me put in the extra effort needed to overcome it. I spent nearly all my time studying, reciting, and practicing.

During my college summer breaks, when I wasn't on a road trip with my family, I worked in the Trout-Goodpine office of the Dallas-based Hunt Petroleum Corporation, where Daddy worked as an oil field consultant. I mostly filed or helped with computer work. One year, I also worked in a hospital laboratory, observing the emergency room doctors with interest.

One summer, I needed to have a few days off to go to an appointment to see Dr. Vargo in Houston. When I told Daddy's secretary I would be away, she asked if Daddy was going with me.

"No, Mama is taking me," I answered.

"It's nice your mother is taking you this year," she said with a smile, seeming as if she was surprised by my plans.

I was taken aback by her response, and thought for a moment, crafting my reply in my head. "Mama takes me to all of my medical appointments," I said. "Daddy hasn't been to any routine appointments since they separated."

"Uh…your father takes time off every year to take you to your checkup," she said with confusion in her voice.

"I don't even go every year," I quipped as I walked out of the room.

Even though Daddy had continued with some of his shady behavior, I really did try to connect with him on the job. One day, I asked Daddy to explain the calculations he did by hand every day. He drew a picture and told me that he needed to determine how far a pipe had deviated from the center of the hole they were drilling, based on the length of pipe and angle at which they drilled.

I listened intently and then designed a spreadsheet that would do the trigonometric calculations for him. Daddy had never completed high school, and though he didn't understand the mathematical theory behind the calculations, he got the general concept. I left work that day feeling a little more connected to him. I could see a bit more of Daddy in me.

***

I never looked forward to my birthday when I was growing up because it coincided with the anniversary of my parents' separation. It dredged up too many bad memories, and my mother always seemed sad and bitter, though she tried hard not to be. In 1997, as I started my sophomore year of college, my twentieth birthday approached. I had no desire to celebrate it. I believed it would be my last. I had never forgotten what Dr. Vargo told Mama during one of my childhood visits to his office about how his oldest patient with Tetralogy of Fallot was in his twenties. All I heard was that my life would end at twenty; as my birthday approached, I never questioned the validity of my childhood assumption. Anything after my birthday, it seemed, was just borrowed time.

Mama always suspected that my early failures in school were an effort to get attention. She told me that I could get as much attention by doing well as I could by doing badly. Her words of wisdom stuck with me. I knew I wanted my life to matter and that I wanted to be remembered for something. Even though I thought I would never live long enough to become a practicing physician, I wanted people to assume I would have become a doctor if I had only lived long enough.

I was headed to Dallas with Matt for a high school football game the weekend before my "doomsday" birthday, depressed. I'd found myself pulling away from almost everyone and everything, including church. I had become a bit reclusive over the next six months. I didn't want to talk about what I was feeling. I thought it best just to focus on schoolwork and not much else. This sudden withdrawal led to some speculation by friends who really cared about me. There were rumors I was drinking heavily. There were theories tossed around that perhaps I was upset that Matt and Tiffany were dating.

None of it was true. My twentieth birthday came and went, and to my surprise, I was still alive. But now I felt immensely lost. I knew it would sound crazy if I said it out loud. *How could someone in his right mind bemoan the fact that he had more days ahead of him?* But I had always planned my life on a twenty-year scale. I had made no plans for life beyond my twentieth birthday. Eventually, I decided that God had given me a little "lagniappe"— a Louisiana word for "something extra." Best described, my time beyond the age of twenty was an unexpected bonus. I would be here for as long as God had purpose for me, so I'd best quit worrying about it.

Another three years would pass and I would be a first-year medical student anticipating another open-heart operation before I realized that Dr. Vargo didn't mean to imply that his patient had *died* at twenty years of age. In fact, the patient Dr. Vargo referred to all those years ago had likely continued to age and would now be nearing his fifth decade of life. This was the first time I realized patients with my condition were living longer than their twenties. Three events would occur over the next year that would ultimately shape my view of the extra time I had been given and teach me to be grateful for it.

The first was that my paternal cousin, Chris Harmon, died in an accident. Chris was my Aunt Lillie Ann's son. He was just eight years older than me. He had always been healthy and very into sports. His death was a shock to all of us and I took it really hard.

Chris had always been one of my favorite cousins, even though he grew up in the Memphis area. The fact that he was gone began to open my eyes to how blessed I was to be alive.

While at Tech, I made friends with two brothers, Nathan and Nick Darby, who, like Chris, also grew up near Memphis. They both played football. I met Nathan in my medical terminology class. He often invited me to his home to grill out and watch sports. Nathan also had an interest in autocross races, and he invited me to come with him to a few races. In autocross, cars didn't race head to head; only one car was on the course at a time. Many of these races were held in empty parking lots with the course laid out by traffic cones. The goal was to complete the course in the fastest time.

Both Nathan and his brother Nick became good friends of mine. Nick would occasionally ask me to go out with him and his friends on the weekends. He knew I wasn't a drinker, so it was only natural for me to be the designated driver. I probably would have never gone to any college parties if it hadn't been for the two of them.

I visited Nick and Nathan at their family's home during summer breaks. They worked as cabana boys at one of the casino resort's pools near their home. One day, hanging out at the resort, I noticed a "Where are they now?" article on the *Growing Pains* cast in a magazine left by the pool. I was happy to catch up on the lives of my favorite childhood TV family and look through photos of the cast both now and on the set. I learned that Jeremy had gone skydiving and enjoyed cooking for his family and friends. I was glad that he was doing well, but I wished that he and I hadn't lost contact when the sitcom ended. I thought briefly about trying to reconnect but decided against it. Why risk altering my memories of such a great day in my life?

My friendship with the Darby brothers gave me the opportunity to stay connected with my Aunt Lillie Ann. I would often make an effort to visit her when I made the trip to Memphis to see Nick and Nathan. One night at dinner Aunt Lillie Ann told me that her grandparents had multiple "blue babies" who had died in infancy. Her grandparents had given birth to four babies who didn't survive. But rather than giving up, Alonzo and Alma Sandifer had gone on to have a healthy son and six healthy daughters. Their daughter Rachel would become my paternal grandmother. I wanted to know more about these babies who would have been my great-aunts and great-uncles. Knowing they had lived gave me a sense of what my fate could have been if I had been born as a "blue baby" before a time when open-heart surgery was possible. Knowing about these relatives who never made it reinforced my feeling that I had been given extra time here for a reason.

The second turn in my attitude came during my junior year, when Grandma Wagoner had quadruple coronary bypass surgery at St. Luke's Episcopal Hospital, a facility adjacent to Texas Children's Hospital. She was in her nineties at the time and had traveled from Central Louisiana to Houston by ambulance. If she needed heart surgery, she wanted to have it where I'd had mine.

Brenda drove me to Houston to visit her in recovery. While there, Grandma asked to see my scar from my heart surgery. Before I even realized what she was doing, Grandma opened her gown to show me hers. I don't think I had ever been so red in the face. Happy she was alive, I chalked up her behavior to the pain medication. She denied it ever happened when I asked her about it later.

I noticed the doctor's name on the room next to Grandma's: "Cooley." I inquired at the nurses' station if this was one of Dr.

Denton Cooley's sons, and I was told it was *the* world-renowned Dr. Denton Cooley himself. He had performed over 100,000 surgeries during his career, I explained, so he probably wouldn't remember me, but he had repaired my Tetralogy of Fallot when I was only two. A little while later, his assistant came to Grandma's room and offered me the opportunity to meet Dr. Cooley, saying that he always liked to see his old patients.

It was the first time I met him, even though he had operated on me as a baby. I went to his clinic on the first floor, where he met with me between patients. He seemed genuinely interested in my life and my plans for the future. One of the things he asked me was "How is your mother?" I'm sure he didn't truly remember her, but it was very endearing that he would ask. He even scribbled a few notes down in a chart about meeting me, saying that he likes to keep records of these things. Getting to shake his hand and thank him was an inspiring milestone in my life.

A man named George Perkins contacted me through the Internet in 1998 during my junior year at Louisiana Tech and asked me to correspond with his eight-year-old son, Ben. The boy was from Los Angeles, and he also had Tetralogy of Fallot. George explained that Ben had begun to deal with his own mortality. Ben had had a successful heart surgery when he was just eleven months old. As he grew up, though, he began to have trouble dealing with the fact that he had been born with a bad heart. He started slipping into a deep depression, unequipped as a child to deal with these issues.

George and his wife Judy were determined to save their son. George was working in Canada as a television and film producer at the time, so he decided to find a job at home in Los Angeles. Judy made plans for Ben to start seeing a psychiatrist. And Ben's doctor at UCLA Medical Center encouraged the family to find someone whom Ben could talk to who had had or was going through a similar experience. That someone was me, though at the time, they didn't know it.

At first the Perkins family had hoped to find someone who was roughly Ben's age. They made contact with a young boy and set up a play date. But Ben and the boy didn't connect. They were too young and didn't have the tools to talk about their concerns and fears with each other.

I had joined a website for congenital heart disease survivors and created a profile page. George sent out messages, hoping someone would respond. Once I did, Ben and I started talking on the phone on a regular basis. And if I wasn't home when he called, Mama would talk to Ben. There was an instant connection. Our friendship was reciprocal. He had lots of questions that I really enjoyed answering. Rather than focusing on medical detail he asked about my life, the things I enjoyed doing as a kid, and where I was headed in life now. I knew that by asking about me, he was gathering information about his condition in his own way, and I was giving him hope that he could make it into his twenties, as well. I think I was able to show Ben he wasn't alone in the world and that I related to what he was going through.

Ben felt different from everyone else. It was a physical difference that made him feel limited and often not healed. His parents didn't know how to normalize things for him and make him feel okay—that's where I came in. Ben's condition was not as extreme as mine. Every patient with Tetralogy of Fallot is different. Being born almost fifteen years later than I was, he benefited from advances in medicine and knowledge gained from previously repaired patients. Ben only had one surgery, and to this day hasn't had to undergo as many procedures. Still, he felt if he pushed too hard he would hurt himself.

Ben helped me realize that I had something to offer other patients with congenital heart defects. I knew if Ben and I both wrestled with thoughts of our own mortality at such a young age, then so did others. It solidified the idea that I was uniquely qualified to pursue a career in pediatric cardiology.

What I wouldn't realize until after I had completed my formal training and had been practicing for a few years is that my less-than-perfect family situation would also give me insight. I see many of the struggles I faced play out in the lives of my patients—even my patients who have never had heart surgery are not immune to the effects of an emotionally hurt heart. When I see kids in my practice with structurally normal hearts who complain of chest pain and palpitations, I have to be cognizant that a bully at school, a family situation they can't control, or some other emotional stressor may be the source of their complaint. I strive to be the "lagniappe" that makes a difference in my patients' lives and let them know they are not alone.

CHAPTER TEN

THE BIG INTERVIEW

D addy took it upon himself to help provide me with financial support to buy books and an occasional meal off campus. There was no longer a court order telling him what he had to do. The things he did from this point forward were because he wanted to, and that made me feel good. He gave me a car and made it possible for me to work at his company during my summer breaks. He even took the time to drive to Ruston to attend occasional award ceremonies.

Those were a few of the things that pointed to the fact that things were improving between us. Yes, I knew they were things that any supportive parent would do for his son, but I appreciated and noticed every last effort. Still, I felt like an outsider in his life. We didn't share similar interests the way my friend Matt and his father did. I still longed for reassurance that he loved me and was proud of me.

Daddy and I took another step toward mending our relationship during my psychology course. In this class, I learned about Pavlov's law on conditioning behavior. Pavlov was a scientist in the 1800s who discovered that behaviors could be triggered by signals. In his famous experiments, he would ring a bell, present a plate of food to a hungry dog, and the dog would salivate in anticipation of what was to come. After a series of repetitions, Pavlov discovered he could ring the bell and the dog would salivate whether or not food was presented. Pavlov's law presents the now well-known theory that a response is an effect of a particular stimulus. After learning about it, I designed my own experiment based on this principle—a test of my relationship with Daddy. I called it "the love experiment."

The love experiment was born from the disturbing fact that I never remembered Daddy telling me he loved me during my childhood. As part of the experiment, I committed to calling Daddy twice a week for a solid month. Each time I did, I made sure to end our telephone conversation by telling him that I loved him. No matter how short or long the call was or what the subject matter was, those would be my last words to him—not just a casual "love ya," but a full-fledged "I love you."

Throughout the month, he never told me that he loved me in return; we just hung up afterward. I can't say that I expected him to respond. In truth, sometimes I wondered if he'd even heard it before he hung up. After the month was over, I called him, ending the conversation with just a "goodbye."

As I went to hang up the phone, I heard him ask, "Don't you love me today?"

I put the phone back to my ear. "I love you every day," I answered back. "I...I just need to...hear those words from *you* every now and then without me having to say them first."

"Well," he responded quietly, "I do love you." He wasn't one to discuss his emotions, but I knew that lesson in honesty had worked on him. From that point on, he would occasionally tell me that he loved me, which was very satisfying to hear. Pavlovian theories aside, it seemed being honest and direct had finally worked.

Daddy just had his own way of doing things. When my sister, Brenda, and her son Jared moved to Monroe, Daddy used to drop off money and canned goods at the door of her apartment and leave without even saying hello. In many ways, this was reminiscent of how he would leave money for me in my car visor while I was at Tech. He didn't hang around long enough to visit or be seen. It wasn't all that different from Santa, minus the magical fireplaces. Maybe we should have left milk and cookies to delay him and to trick him into spending some time with us.

For whatever reason, Daddy dealt with his kids with some built-in distance. I know that now. And in my own way I forgive him for that. I couldn't change him at his core, I eventually realized; I would just have to do my best and love him as he was. Sometimes I wish Mama had not been determined to point out all of Daddy's shortcomings. For example, if I received a birthday card from Daddy, Mama made sure I knew he didn't actually write the inscription on the card or sign it himself. Now I was a pretty observant kid. I noticed everything Daddy did without being told. Her highlighting things like this for me just confirmed what I was thinking and ultimately made me feel worse. But these things happen; this is how children become the handkerchief tied to the middle of the rope in the tug-of-war of divorce.

When I was applying to medical school, Daddy made a point of saying I should go to Tulane because his boss had said that it was a good school. Tulane was my first choice; it had a stellar reputation and fit more with the kind of work I wanted to do. The two public medical schools in the state had a mission to return students to their home community to practice medicine, but I'd never wanted to be just a physician; I wanted to be a pediatric cardiologist like Dr. Vargo. And my many trips to Houston as a child had impressed upon me the idea that pediatric cardiology was a rare medical specialty that couldn't be practiced just anywhere.

But in reality, I had never truly researched the field. I didn't think I would live long enough to practice medicine so the details didn't seem to matter so much as shooting for the loftiest goal possible. When Daddy asked me how much longer I would have to go to school to be a pediatric cardiologist or how much I could expect to earn, I could only give him estimates. He was unimpressed with my estimate of $80,000 a year, considering how much schooling was required. But it seemed like a lot of money to me compared with what Mama had made working as a correctional officer. She had managed to raise me on so much less.

Daddy then took it upon himself to talk to the local hospital in Jena to see if they would help pay my tuition in exchange for an agreement that I would return to practice medicine. I was initially upset that he would speak to the hospital's administration on my behalf without asking me; I wasn't interested in practicing in Jena at all. It is only with years of hindsight that I have come to realize that he was only trying to help. I am sure the prospect of my going to medical school and incurring a significant amount of debt was overwhelming to him. He hadn't anticipated this issue, and he wanted to help me avoid the debt he thought would be a burden to me.

I began interviewing at several medical schools in the state, including Louisiana State University Health Sciences Center, but I really set my sights on Tulane University School of Medicine. Factoring into my consideration, however, was the school's $100 application fee and disclaimer that anyone hoping to join its class of 150 students should consider the odds of actually being accepted from a pool of nearly 10,000 applicants. This was enough to keep me from placing stamps on the envelope containing my application until Wayne declared he would give the money back to me if I didn't at least get a chance to interview.

I am still so grateful for Wayne's generosity. Soon after sending my application to Tulane, I received a thin envelope in the mail; to my surprise, it contained an invitation to come visit the school. On the day of my interview, I met with Dr. Paul Rodenhauser, assistant dean for academic and counseling services. His title, though long and quite impressive, does not exist today; once he retired, the job he did for Tulane was eventually divided among four people. Clearly, that says a lot about the man I would come to know. When I met him, his role was to keep up with and advise the medical school's students, while prescreening others who wanted to become students. I was one of the latter, seated across from him, eager to answer his every question, determined to get them all right.

During enrollment season, Dr. Rodenhauser interviewed on average twenty applicants per week for the university before sending his recommendations on to the school's dean of admissions for final consideration. The good doctor had a practice of not reading through applicant portfolios in advance to avoid any preconceived notions or expectations. This allowed him to base his impressions on what the applicant was willing to talk about and then judge that against their actual demeanor. Certainly Dr. Rodenhauser took into account academic accomplishments, but his initial focus was solely on the person seated in front of him.

So he had no idea about me or my history before our first encounter. I am sure he had experienced applicants like me before—those fresh out of college, anxious to begin life as med students, on their way to an exciting practice that would enable them to heal the world. My anxiousness, however, was focused on the issue of life and death. Unlike other candidates who were "dying" to get into this prestigious school, I was just grateful to be alive and unsure of how much time I had left on this earth.

He began by asking me to talk about myself. I remember feeling very at ease with him for the next half hour.

He asked tough questions about my family and background. "How do you relate to your family members—the fact that they are less formally educated than you?"

"I don't value people by the degrees they hold," I answered.

But that's not what Dr. Rodenhauser was really getting at. He explained that sometimes when only one family member is a high achiever, it can cause stress in ways I couldn't imagine. If I was being honest with myself, I thought, my ambition and drive had already driven a wedge between my father and me. It was certainly no reason not to have goals, but I could understand Dr. Rodenhauser's point.

"How would you cope if you got to Tulane and weren't at the very top of your class?" he asked. "Everyone here is very bright, and not everyone can be number one."

I talked about my early failures in school. He asked when I began to do well in school, and that is when I told my story about Starlight Children's Foundation and how getting to visit the set of *Growing Pains* had been a turning point for me. I put everything out on the table, giving him my life story—specifically, my medical history and how I was born with a heart defect.

I was willing to share things about myself that others may have withheld, and I think that impressed him. On the way out of our interview, he pointed out the anatomy specimens on display in the hallways near the gross anatomy labs, and I marveled at the embryology museum, which I toured before I left.

Only later would I find out the full extent of the concerns Dr. Rodenhauser had upon interviewing me. The school had accepted students in the past with chronic illnesses, and they hadn't been able to complete the program. He wondered if my heart condition could prevent me from finishing what I started, thus taking away a spot from another potential applicant. It was a serious consideration as he prepared my file for further ranking by Tulane's admissions committee. However, he made it a practice not to allow conditions like cystic fibrosis or Tetralogy of Fallot or major depressive disorder to stand in the way of recommending a qualified student for admission. After all, these same students had already excelled in stressful college courses. He expected that individuals with health issues would take the stress factor into consideration, that they would find an equally stressful challenge in another school if not accepted, and that their stress level might even be increased by not being able to pursue their dream of being a physician. As he did in all his professional duties he worked thoughtfully, consistently, and impartially when considering applicants.

The day I interviewed at Tulane was October 21—Jeremy Miller's birthday. I thought about Jeremy on the day of my interview and wondered where his life had taken him. In retrospect I realized that the date of my interview was not a coincidence. It was the first in a series of events that would bring me closer to my childhood wish than I could have ever imagined.

There was just something about the place that was so impressive; I felt deep down that it was where I should be. Most of my friends were going to LSU; it was less expensive and closer to home. But I began to have recurring dreams about Tulane and those anatomy specimens almost every night following my visit. I eventually went and asked one of my trusted science faculty at Tech where I should go. He told me that he would tell most students in my position to go to LSU, but he felt I should choose Tulane. He thought I would do well with the diversity there. It fit well with what I felt inside—what it seemed like God was telling me to do.

I received my acceptance about a week after my interview in October 1999. I picked up my mail on the way to class. I opened it at the post office but then immediately went to Dr. Ramu's physical chemistry class. I could barely sit still with excitement! I shared the news with him after class. Then I called my mom on the cell phone I had only in case of emergency; it had only ten minutes a month on it, for use if I had car trouble on the way to class. But if anything was worth using up my minutes, my acceptance to medical school was. She needed to know!

***

As my college graduation approached and I could feel my dream of going to medical school coming closer to fruition, I posted online about my wish experience and how much the T-shirt Kirk Cameron had signed with the words "God bless you!" meant to me. Later, I received an email from an acquaintance of Kirk's, telling me about a weeklong, all-expenses-paid retreat for terminally ill children and their families called Camp Firefly. The message went on to say that Camp Firefly is a charity started by Kirk Cameron and his wife Chelsea because of their interaction with wish kids on the *Growing Pains* set. The author of the email said that Kirk would be interested in hearing about my life and provided the number for Camp Firefly.

I wasn't able to call for some time; I simply didn't have the time. I was focused entirely on passing my finals. I already had my acceptance to medical school in hand, which had taken off some of the pressure, but I was trying to maintain a perfect 4.0 and really didn't want to throw things off at the last moment. But the day before my college graduation, I finally got enough time—and got up enough nerve—to call the number.

A man answered the phone, and I began to introduce myself. "Hi, my name is Brandon. I received an email about Camp Firefly, and I was told to call and share my story. I visited with Kirk Cameron on the set of *Growing Pains* when I had a wish granted..." I trailed off, wanting to make sure someone was still on the line.

There was a pause, and then the man said, "Brandon, this is me, Kirk."

He had answered the phone at his own charity! I couldn't believe it. Kirk and I talked for about ten minutes. He was so personable that I felt as though I were talking to an old friend—or to Mike Seaver himself, I thought happily. Kirk was in Canada, filming the first *Left Behind* movie. He said that *Growing Pains* was a platform that God had used to allow him to reach the lost. He even told me about his children. Kirk ended the call by giving me his manager's email address and telling me to keep in touch.

When I hung up the phone, I thought about my wish and the conversation I'd had with Kirk on the set of *Growing Pains* over a decade before. God had used the experience then to answer my prayer and to show me that He loved me despite all of the challenges in my young life. I knew when I hung up the phone that the timing of this conversation wasn't a coincidence. This was the first time I'd had any communication with a cast member since *Growing Pains* had stopped filming. I realized that something big was about to happen in my life, and God wanted me to know that He loved me and He was in control. All afternoon I thought about my conversation with Kirk, trying to figure out its purpose.

The next day I graduated summa cum laude from Louisiana Tech with a 4.0-grade-point average. Daddy and his wife were in the audience, along with Mama and Brenda. My childhood friend, Jarred Pugh, and some other former high school classmates I still kept in touch with came to see me walk across the stage to receive my diploma and a medal for my academic accomplishments. I know Mama was proud. I finally felt as though Daddy was, too. I suppose my joy over having reached another major milestone is what made me ask my parents if we could *all* go to dinner together. Daddy flat-out refused; sitting at a table with Mama was not his idea of a celebration. I was stung that he could not make the effort to join me to celebrate such an important accomplishment, but I tried not to show my disappointment. Just being present was all he could manage, and because it was so much more than he had done at other times in my life, I just had to accept it for what it was.

All through my summer break, I had a recurring dream that the *Growing Pains* cast would be at my white coat ceremony, in which each incoming medical student dons a short, white medical coat for the first time and shares with their classmates what they hope to bring to their practice of medicine.

Of course, the *Growing Pains* cast wasn't there during the ceremony, when I boldly told my classmates that I wanted to bring Christ to my patients as Mama looked on. But they eventually came back into my life as I had dreamed they would. They would be there for an important milestone in every medical student's career—the day I found out where I would go after Tulane, when I would learn my childhood dream was finally coming to fruition.

They would be there for me when Daddy no longer could.

CHAPTER ELEVEN

AN UNEXPECTED TRIP TO
THE OPERATING ROOM

"Look to your left; now, look to your right. One of you will not be here come graduation." It's the cliché speech given in nearly every movie about med school, always pointed out loudly by a professor standing in front of a stadium-sized auditorium with wall-to-wall med students. The camera zooms in on the faces of fearful would-be doctors, already feeling the pressure to *make it* as a physician.

Tulane had a reputation for making sure that scene didn't happen. They were selective in the beginning, but almost all the students who enrolled in their program made it through. I liked this about Tulane; it made me feel as though they were making a serious investment in me. As for the venue, medical school for me and my class didn't start in that terrifyingly large auditorium like in the movies. It began as an overnight orientation at nearby Camp Tchefuncte. In what's known as one of the most unique and beautiful settings in Louisiana, the camp is characterized by tall pines, beds of yellow flowers, and campground-style cabins. The Tchefuncte River runs lazily through the grounds, and at night the hum of tree frogs and mosquitoes is the only thing that breaks the heavy silence.

We spent the first night listening to music and having drinks while getting to know each other. The next day we were encouraged to play team-building games to get to know each other better. It was over the course of these two days that I met Dr. Hosea Doucet, a member of the pediatric faculty at Tulane. He was interested in learning how I knew I wanted to be a pediatric cardiologist before I had even started learning human anatomy. I told him my story. He listened with great interest and then generously arranged for me to meet with Dr. Robert Ascuitto when I returned to campus. Dr. Ascuitto was a pediatric cardiologist at Tulane University Medical Center.

When I met him, Dr. Ascuitto asked about my intentions for study. Then abruptly, he changed the subject and asked me if I had a pulmonary valve. I told him that I thought it had been removed during my first heart surgery. He then asked if I would mind if he did a quick echocardiogram.

That's not something you hear every day: "Can I just do a quick echocardiogram on you?" I'd thought I was just going to meet Dr. Ascuitto because I had an interest in his field. But rather than getting questions on how I wanted my coffee, like a normal visiting student might have, he wanted to perform an echocardiogram. I shrugged and agreed. It's not like my life has ever been normal anyway.

After the unsolicited examination and to my complete surprise, Dr. Ascuitto said it was in my best interest to leave medical school and have a second heart surgery to implant an artificial pulmonary valve into my heart. The type of repair I'd undergone as a child, he explained, had since been proven to have adverse effects on the heart in the long run. Treatment options had evolved, and he felt a new competent valve would serve me better in the long term. He suggested that I consider having the surgery at Mayo Clinic in Minnesota, explaining that once I healed, there would be no problem in my returning to Tulane the following year. "No problem," he finished. "You have to take care of yourself before you can take care of anyone else."

No problem?! No one knew how hard I had worked to get to medical school. Now I was expected to leave it before it really even began?

I understood Dr. Doucet's reasoning for arranging the checkup at Tulane. It was out of concern for me. Still, I couldn't help but resent his timing. I was miles away from home and left to make this decision on my own.

I called Mama with the news, and she suggested I call Dr. Vargo for guidance. I had just seen him a few months earlier for a checkup and he had sent me on my way with a positive report, telling me to go and enjoy New Orleans.

Dr. Vargo wasn't available when I called, so I left a message for him to call me.

When I arrived home a few hours later, I noticed the light blinking on my answering machine. *"This is Tom. Call me,"* said the voice on the tape. I didn't know any Toms, so I assumed the message must have been left for whoever owned my number previously. It took me a few days to realize it was Dr. Vargo. He had always signed his letters Thomas A. Vargo, MD, and in more familiar, face-to-face moments he was simply Dr. Vargo.

While I was waiting to hear back from him, though, dark thoughts started to gather on the horizon of my mind. I should probably just quit school. I worried about incurring the massive debt of a medical education only to find myself unable to finish. I worried about the effects of stress and exhaustion on my health. If I couldn't even make it through the first week of class without needing surgery, this might not be for me. And in any case, was all this worth it? Did I really want to go through the time and stress of medical school if my dreams of becoming a doctor might never come to fruition anyway?

I walked over to the Office of Student Affairs to gather information on what my next steps should be if I did decide to withdraw from medical school. There I met Charlotte Steger, the registrar for the school. I was struck immediately by her maternal presence. You could tell she cared for the med students. Charlotte was someone God used to guide me and make me feel as if I wasn't all alone in my decision making. She ended up being a real blessing during my time at Tulane. When I explained to Charlotte what was going on with my health and why I was inquiring about withdrawing from school, she offered some sound advice.

"You should at least enroll in the first semester," she insisted. "You haven't paid tuition yet, so if you withdraw now, it will be like you were never a student here. You'll have to reapply to the medical school program without any guarantees you'll be accepted a second time!"

Charlotte encouraged me to go ahead and pay my tuition and then take a leave of absence if needed. I was almost convinced. I told her I'd think about it and let her know for sure.

Once I realized he was the mysterious "Tom," Dr. Vargo and I finally connected on the phone. "There are gray areas in medicine. Often, two physicians can look at the same data and come to completely different, but both valid, conclusions," he explained. He was the type of man who was conservative in his practice of medicine; he erred on the side of caution with relatively new advances such as the pulmonary valve, and in his own practice he wanted to see more studies and long-term results before recommending it to more patients. But he agreed that Mayo Clinic would be a good choice for a second opinion, and he arranged to have my medical records sent there for review.

News of my potential summer plans traveled fast around campus. It wasn't long before I was called into the office of Dr. Joseph Pisano, the dean of admissions, to talk about my surgery. Like everyone else I had encountered at Tulane, he was very supportive. He told me the admissions committee hadn't selected me because of what I had done. I was chosen because of what they felt *I had the potential of doing.* This was a stunning revelation. Dr. Pisano was trying to tell me he was doing the same thing Dr. Rodenhauser had done during my initial interview: He was looking beyond my heart defect.

Finally, Mayo Clinic wrote that they agreed that I should have a pulmonary valve implanted. They felt we could delay the surgery to the summer between my first and second year of medical school. The summer surgery date meant I wouldn't miss any time from school, and the fact that it would be after my first year made reapplying to Tulane a nonissue. This was a welcome blessing.

I checked into Mayo Clinic in Rochester, Minnesota, in the summer of 2001 for an open-heart surgery that was performed by Dr. Francisco Puga. I had a full checkup the day before my surgery. Daddy and his wife had driven to Minnesota. Wayne had generously bought plane tickets for Brenda, Mama, and me several months before so that I would not have to make the trip back to Louisiana in a car. This gift would be the last he ever gave me; unfortunately, kind Wayne died of complications from a stroke just a few months before I had surgery.

On the day before my surgery, I instinctively tried to plan

lunch with Daddy and dinner with Mama to avoid conflict. But Mama would not have it. She insisted that she would not be apart from me on this day. Daddy had no choice but to join us or miss out on being with me. It is the only time that I could remember both my parents and my sister sitting down for a meal together since Mama and Daddy's divorce some twenty years earlier. It was a bit awkward, and I could not help thinking back on how my father had refused to have dinner with us after my graduation, but everyone seemed to set aside their differences. Lunch went well enough that we repeated it for dinner at the Old Country Buffet that evening. Once we returned to Jena, of course, it was like it never happened, but at the time the only downside was that the day had to end.

That night was one of the longest I can remember. I knew just enough from my anatomy class to worry about the possible risks of the surgery, and I could not stop going over all the things that could go wrong. Even beyond the surgery itself, I worried that the drama in my family would build to a breaking point. I focused on the presurgical prep I had been assigned: I had to put antibiotic ointment in my nose to reduce the risk of infection and wash the surgical site with a special type of soap. Then I lay awake for what felt like forever. The only thing I knew for sure, I realized helplessly, was that life would be a lot different after tomorrow.

***

I woke up in the ICU to find Chris Janssen sitting in my room. Chris was one of my classmates at Tulane. Our relationship grew as we began to study together during our first year in med school. Class attendance was not mandatory for many courses at Tulane; there was a note-taking service available, and most of my classmates and I chose to study instead of attending class when possible. Chris and I would meet almost every day to study together in the library. We would read through small amounts of material and then quiz each other on it. During exam week, we would meet at 8:00 a.m., break for an hour lunch, and then study for another four hours before going to the gym. Then, every night we would end with another study session from 7:00 p.m. until midnight. Some could say Chris and I overdid it, but there were so many demands and so much stress on us that we actually benefited from having each other—not just as study partners, but as friends. Where I was organized and methodical, he lived his life a bit more spontaneous and unstructured. What we have always had in common is our desire to learn and a willingness to put in the time. I was also nervous at the thought of my upcoming surgery and needed someone I could just relax with (even if relaxing consisted of quizzing each other on anatomy terms).

Waking up in the ICU to find my good friend Chris was a real blessing—and quite a surprise, since it was my understanding that only family was allowed in the ICU. Chris jokingly told me that Mama had told the hospital staff he was my brother. Chris was a six-foot-five-inch, 230-pound ex-football player. I guess the nurses didn't notice our physical differences. In any case, Chris had driven from South Dakota to be with me during my surgery; there was no way he was going to let a few hospital rules stop him. In fact, "Brother Chris" would later be the one who pushed me in a wheelchair from the ICU to my hospital room after surgery.

Looking back on this, I have come to realize that my friendship with Chris was not an accident. Chris had spent his college years at Augustana University in South Dakota. Mayo Clinic has one of the smallest medical school classes in the country, and it just so happened that one of his best friends from college, John, was a medical student there. Even after Chris left town following my surgery, John continued to check on me. What are the odds that out of my medical school class of 150 people, I would become friends with the guy who had a friend at Mayo Clinic who could care for me? My first year of medical school was filled with anxious anticipation for my upcoming surgery, and my return to school the following year had its own set of challenges. Chris was the friend I needed to help me through both.

Today, Chris is a pain specialist. He did his residency at Northwestern in Chicago and his fellowship at UCLA in Los Angeles. He attributes some of his success to me, saying I helped keep him organized during our first two years of med school. Throughout the time we spent together, Chris never seemed to notice any of my physical difficulties, even though we discussed my health several times as my surgery approached. He was supportive but treated me like a normal person, which I always appreciated.

I've heard the stories of who was present at my first open-heart surgery when I was a baby and how I was surrounded by faith and love. I don't remember the pain or the family members who were there; I'll have to take their word for it. But when it came to this second surgery, there are things I'll never forget. What sticks with me most is the way I was able to move from fear and uncertainty to faith and hope. Once again, I was surrounded by love—Mama, Daddy, Brenda, other members of my family, and friends like Chris Janssen were there for me.

Trey Robertson, my childhood friend from Jena who is also the son of my pastor, Brother Bill, unknowingly played a role in my surgery and recovery, as well. He and his wife Staci welcomed their first son, Will, into the world on the very day I had my surgery. Will's birthday on Facebook is my yearly reminder of my surgery's anniversary and how hard I worked to overcome it.

I learned a lot recovering from my second open-heart surgery. I discovered a need for true compassion. It started with the number of cards and gifts I received from my Tulane classmates. I must have received close to a hundred different items in the mail at my home, wishing me well in the early days that followed my surgery. I was overwhelmed by the compassion of my classmates; it was as though I had gained an extended family of 150 people in the last year. I looked forward to checking the mailbox every day, and I needed what I found in it. The healing process can be such an internal, solitary thing. I didn't discover the extent of that until the packages finally stopped coming, and I was only left with time on my hands to recover.

Initially, every movement hurt. Transitioning from lying down to sitting up was difficult. I had a pillow to hold against my breast bone when I coughed. (Not only was my heart healing, but my breast bone had been cracked open to get to my heart, so I was healing from the break, too.) And as bad as coughing was, sneezing was worse; to this day, I cringe when I sneeze.

But for the most part my pain was easily controlled. The downtime was the problem. For months after my surgery I felt aimless and alone. I was not allowed to drive for four weeks, so I hung aimlessly around the house. I would not go with my mother to visit Grandma in the nursing home, as I was afraid of getting an infection in my healing wounds. I hung around Brenda's newly opened store in Jena, which sold knickknacks, just looking for people with whom to talk. As soon as I got the okay, I visited my friends Nathan and Nick in Memphis, desperately wanting life to return to normal.

What I didn't see coming was how difficult it was for me to

return to Tulane to start my second year. I felt like I had been robbed of my summer break. My classmates had traveled the world and done amazing things in their time off. In contrast, I felt drained and depressed. I didn't feel like I belonged in medical school or anywhere else. I found it hard to study or even go to the gym with Chris.

I came to realize that the second operation had blindsided me in regard to my plans for the future. It wasn't something I had planned. I started to wonder if I could truly break free from the hospital room and step back into the classroom. Even if I did, I could only imagine what other surprises were in store for me regarding my health. I had the drive to succeed, but the idea that there might always be obstacles made me feel bitter and angry. Couldn't I ever move forward without being set back by my heart? Would I continue to be held a prisoner by my condition for the rest of my life? The whole thing brought me back to grade school and how isolated I felt from the other kids my age.

Dr. Rodenhauser encouraged me to write about my feelings. He checked on me often and assured me that my feelings were normal given the circumstances. With time and good counsel, my emotions healed in the same way my body did. Some positives came from the second heart surgery. It taught me about the healing effect of compassion from all those cards and gifts that came to my house. It removed certain physical restrictions from my life, including enabling me to stop relying on my daily dose of digoxin. I also wrote an article called "Skydiving" with Dr. Rodenhauser's help. "Skydiving" appeared in the *Journal of the American Medical Association* in July 2002. It compared my life's journey to falling out of the sky with a parachute. Considering everything I had been through and was going through, I had proven I was destined to survive, I wrote—I just had to be fearless and, of course, have faith in the impossible. Even publishing that article seemed an impossible feat for someone in just their second year of med school, but I did it.

The following summer, between my second and third year of med school, a young man from Nashville doing an internship with the local newspaper sublet the apartment next to mine in New Orleans. He was a few years younger than me, but occasionally he and I would go out for pizza together. One evening after going out for dinner, he came back to my apartment and noticed the *Growing Pains* T-shirt hung on my living room wall. He began to ask questions about the shirt. I thought he was just another fan like I was. As it turns out, this was another strange coincidence. His father was helping manage Kirk Cameron's speaking career.

***

Through my surgery, I was introduced to Dr. Allison Cabalka. She did my echocardiogram before I was discharged from the hospital. As I chatted with her during the procedure, I learned that Dr. Vargo had played a role in her education when she had trained in pediatric cardiology at Texas Children's Hospital. I was so excited to discover the connection between her and my mentor that I asked if she would become my Minnesota cardiologist.

I had run into a problem. I needed to return to Mayo Clinic for a checkup during my senior year of medical school, but my health insurance was through Tulane, and Mayo Clinic was considered "out of network" for me. But Charlotte Steger came to my aid again! She knew that there was a clause in the insurance policy that would allow me to be seen "in network" at Mayo Clinic if I went there as a visiting medical student for an away rotation. In essence, where you were visiting became your home institution.

She suggested I apply for an away rotation so I wouldn't need to pay the astronomical costs for my care out of pocket.

Knowing this, I called Dr. Cabalka and told her I needed to come for my checkup with her but that I also wanted to spend a month at Mayo Clinic learning from the doctors who had cared for me. Without hesitation, Dr. Cabalka worked it out, and I visited Mayo Clinic in November 2003.

The first thing I was struck by was the cold. This was my first real encounter with snow. I remember one day just standing at the fourth-floor window of the Mary Brigh building, just watching it fall. I was mesmerized.

Mayo Clinic is incredibly impressive, especially the gorgeous, marble-filled Gonda building. But the efficiency of the clinic is its most amazing feature. When patients had their labs drawn, I saw with amazement, the blood was placed on a conveyor belt to be whisked away and processed. If additional tests or appointments were needed they could be set up within a few days, if not the same day. The physicians were full of knowledge and spent a lot of their time teaching. I found myself spending extra time in the clinic, enthralled by the impromptu lectures Dr. David Driscoll gave on the dry erase board. He was one of the most well-read and efficient physicians I had ever encountered. He, too, had trained under Dr. Vargo at Texas Children's Hospital.

The whole month I was there I saw Dr. Puga several times, but I wasn't sure if he remembered me. But one day he sought me out specifically and asked if I could join him. "Of course!" I replied. He took me into a patient's room, and it was clear I was there to be part of his show-and-tell. Dr. Puga had a patient with Tetralogy of Fallot who was reluctant to have pulmonary valve replacement surgery. Dr. Puga wanted her to have an opportunity to ask me questions patient to patient. I gave her details on the pain she should expect and what the recovery would involve, trying to ease her fears as best I could by providing her with information.

When I went back to Mayo as a visiting medical student, I realized that it was because of people who helped guide me through some difficult decisions and others who allowed me to glean opportunities from the experience. Mayo Clinic gave me a scholarship to help cover the cost of staying a month in the Kahler Grand Hotel. Though I didn't realize it at the time, I had no need to worry about lost tuition, medical bills I couldn't pay, or even a place to stay. All of it was provided. In a sense, I had Tulane's dean of admissions, Dr. Vargo, Ms. Steger, Chris Janssen, Dr. Cabalka, Mama, Daddy, and Sissy all sitting at the table with me.

God made sure I was never really alone.

CHAPTER TWELVE

LITERALLY SHARING MY HEART

W hen I began at Tulane, I learned that my 150 classmates and I were to spend two years of medical school focused on classroom studies and another two years on clinical rotations. But starting the second day of class, I found out things would not be as easy as that. Three bumps in the road happened on my way to my medical degree.

The first bump was obviously the diagnosis that necessitated a second heart surgery. That was not a bump, but more of a roadblock. Fortunately, I'd maneuvered around it with the help of family, friends, and Dr. Vargo's guidance and direction. All of that love and support helped me survive the surgery and the depression that followed it during my second year.

Part of what got me through that depression was being able to set an example for my classmates. I met Dr. Elma LeDoux as a first-year student; she would be involved in my education all four years. She is an adult cardiologist and was the director of the third-year internal medicine clerkship while I was a student. During first-year physiology class she taught part of the cardiac block of the course. When she learned about my heart problem through another faculty member, she asked me if I would be willing to come forward and demonstrate the difference between a normal electrocardiogram (ECG) reading and one that was done on a heart that had been through surgery. Eager to gain her respect, I agreed.

The next morning, I found myself in front of my 150 class-mates while Dr. LeDoux placed ECG stickers on my chest, arms, and legs. The stickers connected to wires, which helped the ECG machine measure the heart's electrical activity. Even today, Dr. LeDoux will tell you it was my compliance that impressed her. What was unusual about my agreeing to the demonstration was that most students in medical school don't like to stand out. It is an intimidating environment, filled with intelligent and driven people who don't like to waste time, and long questions or anec-dotes in class are frowned upon. Most would rather hang in the background than be singled out for anything at all. I was no different, but I felt it was important to use my story to educate others. Dr. LeDoux says it was at this point that she discovered the generous part of my character. I had literally shared my heart with my classmates.

Dr. LeDoux taught cardiac physical diagnosis during my sec-ond year, and in my third year, she directed the internal medicine clerkship. During my fourth year, I spent some time working with her in her adult cardiology clinic. It wasn't long into my relation-ship with Dr. LeDoux that we became close and I began to see her as a mentor, though my focus on pediatric cardiology would take me down a slightly different career path. Still, Dr. LeDoux was a part of my journey and the one person who, in my third year, would support me through the second bump I would face at Tulane.

She noticed a dip in my test scores and that historically I did much better on exams written by Tulane's faculty compared to timed, standardized ones. When I told her about my difficulty with reading during my early school days and the fact that I had always struggled with the reading portion of standardized tests, she wondered aloud whether I possibly had an undiagnosed learning disability. She said it was common in people who are born with significant heart defects.

At first, I was insulted and a little defensive. "How could I have graduated at the top of my high school and college classes, then?" I pushed.

"You likely developed unique study skills over time," she replied patiently. "That's how you were able to do so well. Let's have you tested so we know for sure."

"I'll think about it. I really don't think this is necessary," I said and walked out of her office awkwardly, her words stinging the whole way home.

Dr. LeDoux brought it up the next time I saw her, though, and the next. At first, I resisted the testing. I was already known as the student with the heart condition—did I really want the added stigma of being different because of a learning disability?

But she continuously insisted I get tested and even offered to pay for it. She told me it was important because if I did have a learning disability, I may one day need testing accommodations. The way she saw it, a low-scoring test should not be able to dictate my future. I had worked so hard, she argued. Not to take advantage of perfectly reasonable accommodations was jeopardizing my career.

Of course, she was right. I eventually agreed to take the test.

In doing so, I learned I had a significant reading disorder that was limited to reading speed. Even though additional time was recommended for exams, I chose to continue to take my exams under the same conditions as my classmates. I had made it to medical school despite my difficulties with reading, I thought; my system worked. Regardless of the problems I faced with reading, my pride prevented me from accepting the accommodation.

Though I tried to ignore it, however, the testing would ultimately help me in the long run. My third year had brought with it more standardized tests, and as I was unwilling to take the accommodation, my grades suffered as a result. I learned later that when I applied to residency programs, my dean indirectly mentioned my learning disability in his letter of recommendation by sharing that my performance on standardized exams was likely not an accurate reflection of my potential as a physician.

I had succeeded academically in spite of my condition by learning how to study differently—Dr. LeDoux had gotten that correct. Where I had difficulty reading, I compensated by spending the extra time I needed to learn the material. The testing showed that my auditory memory was highly developed; verbally rehearsing facts over and over with Mama as a boy and studying with friends throughout college and med school had helped me do well because I was able to recall the things they called out to me. Where one study skill was underdeveloped, I had used my other skills to make up for it, strengthening my auditory memory through sheer determination.

My third and biggest obstacle appeared on the horizon during my second year of school when Daddy called to let me know he had been diagnosed with metastatic prostate cancer. The doctors were cautiously optimistic at first, but the cancer had spread to his bones. Soon everyone realized what was to come.

The news hit me like a ton of bricks. It was made even more difficult because I realized that time would ultimately prevent Daddy
and me from having the relationship I wanted us to have. Bracing
myself for the way I imagined our relationship would ultimately
end, I did what I had always done throughout my life. I compensated for what would be the loss of my dad by focusing on
my studies and my future goal. In so doing, I overcame my third
roadblock—if only temporarily.

The day before I received my undergraduate degree from
Louisiana Tech, Kirk Cameron and I had spoken by phone when
he was in Canada filming his first *Left Behind* movie. An acquaintance of Kirk's had helped us reconnect after he saw a story I had
posted online about my wish and the T-shirt that the *Growing
Pains* cast had signed for me, sharing how the experience had
given me hope for my future. I had grown to believe that I had
reacquainted with Kirk at that time, just before moving to New
Orleans and starting at Tulane, because God wanted to remind
me through Kirk that He cared for me. He loved me even when I
was facing something big.

My need for a second heart surgery and Daddy's cancer diagnosis were both big enough to shake my faith. I began emailing
Kirk regularly, checking in about my recovery and then about my
dad's illness. Regardless of how busy he was, he always made the
time to reply, and I felt safe sharing my inner thoughts and fears
with him in a way I could not with anyone else. Our friendship
grew during this difficult time. As in my childhood, God seemed
to send him to me as a friend just when I needed him most. It
would not be the last time.

***

Tulane is different from other schools—I can't stress that enough. Dr. Joseph Pisano, dean of admissions, said many times, "If you aren't playing as hard as you are working, you are not doing medical school in New Orleans correctly." I came to realize that was the going theme for the school when, before my first set of exams, while sitting in an all-day review session—eyes glazed over from looking at histology slides—we heard trumpets and a drum playing in the hallway. The next thing we knew, the students from the second-year class rushed through the front and rear doors into the large lecture hall with stadium seating. They started throwing candy and beads, hosting a mini Mardi Gras to help us relax. As I looked around, the tired eyes of my classmates lit up, and we all erupted in laughter. They marched in a circle around the classroom, singing a rewritten version of Gloria Gaynor's "I Will Survive" that referenced histology terms and inside jokes about medical school. The trumpeters and drummer went to town with insane enthusiasm, and they didn't leave until everyone had jumped up to dance, our spirits reinvigorated.

A lot of my Tulane classmates excelled in the arts. As a result, we had regular M&M meetings. M&M in medicine usually means morbidity and mortality. At Tulane, it also means "Music and Medicine." Regularly, classmates and faculty would put on concerts. The lady who delivered mail throughout the school would come play the piano for us sometimes. It was always quite the party! You have not experienced everything medical school can be until you have seen a room full of people in white coats doing the chicken dance. These were among the many things that made Tulane so special and so necessary for where I was in life. The music, fun, and celebration lifted my spirits even when my mind was occupied with dark or heavy thoughts.

Another frequent Dr. Pisano saying to applicants was

"Medical school is not four years out of your life; it is four years *of* your life." My classmates and I were encouraged to make the most of our time at Tulane, both in and out of the classroom, and to improve our community wherever possible. Encouraged by this, I got involved with the Make-A-Wish Foundation. First, I was a volunteer wish granter. Being a wish granter was so much fun. Occasionally, I would get to go to a wish kid's home and ask them those all-important questions: *Who would you want to meet? Where would you want to go?*

I also went on a wish with one of the kids, a teenager suffering from cancer. He initially wanted to appear on the WWF. While it wouldn't have been a problem to have him meet a WWF star, like the Rock, the organization had a policy not to allow the kids on TV because of the number of wish requests they received. The kid settled on some new rims and entertainment system for his truck. Knowing he was a Saints fan, a surprise was arranged. He was picked up in a limo and taken to a Saints practice while the work was being done on his truck. The players greeted him after practice, and his favorite player even gave him his helmet.

Later, I was asked to sit on the board of directors of the Louisiana chapter of Make-A-Wish. During my senior year, I volunteered to be a counselor at Camp Bon Coeur, a summer camp for children born with heart defects, in Lafayette, Louisiana. Children came from all over the country to attend camp. I thought this would be the perfect opportunity to finally meet my pen pal Ben Perkins from California.

I called his parents, George and Judy, and they agreed to allow Ben to come. Ben was eleven at the time. I got to be his counselor while he was at camp. It seemed like a safe way for us to meet face-to-face, considering we had connected on the Internet simply because we shared a diagnosis and the uncertainty about our future that comes with it. Ben had a lot of fun at the camp, which is just like a normal summer camp—with archery, arts and crafts, games, and songs—except it is staffed with nurses and physicians from across the country, and campers can compare scars and stories and really open up about their experiences. Ben made connections with other campers during this time that he still has today.

When I told her Ben was coming to Camp Bon Coeur, Mama decided to come out for family day to finally meet the boy with whom she had shared so many hours on the phone.

"Ms. Phillips, can Brandon visit me in Los Angeles?" Ben asked Mama at lunch, without regard to the fact that I was in my mid-twenties and almost a doctor.

"Of course, he'll go out there and visit you soon!" she replied without thinking.

I sat back in my seat and thought about it. *I never imagined I'd have another excuse to visit L.A. again. … This is a great reason.* Soon enough, I'd be planning my trip.

***

During my senior year of medical school, I began interviewing for a pediatric residency position. Residency lasts three years, and in the interest of working at the best possible hospital, I interviewed all over the country—UCLA, Yale, Tulane, Baylor, and Washington University in St. Louis. It was a time of reflection, as I found myself starting from a place where my choices were being determined by the experiences I'd had as a child. I had always wanted to work with Dr. Vargo, so my obvious first choice was Texas Children's Hospital at Baylor College of Medicine. In addition to having Dr. Vargo, this hospital had one of the top pediatric programs in the country. It was considered an extremely competitive program, and some of Tulane's pediatric faculty considered it a long shot for me, considering students with better test scores and class ranking had not "matched" there in the past.

This was certainly important to consider. Applying for a residency position is much different from applying for medical school. It isn't a matter of being *accepted* by the program; there is a *matching* process. You apply to programs of interest and hope to be invited for an onsite interview. Once you interview, you then rank all the programs that interviewed you in your order of preference. The programs then rank their interviewees in order of preference. A computer algorithm *matches* you with the highest-ranked program on your list that isn't already filled with applicants that the program ranked higher than you. All medical students across the country find out where they will go after medical school on Match Day. Every medical student fears not matching with any program on their list and having to *scramble* for an available program spot that went unfilled in the match process. The competitiveness of Baylor's pediatric program combined with the uncertainty of this matching process caused me to take plenty of time to consider all of my options.

I applied to UCLA in Los Angeles, and I was invited for an interview. I called Ben's family to let them know I would be in the area and wanted to meet them. Ben's family insisted that I stay with them while I was in town. They even offered to let me drive one of their cars while I was there. It was an offer I couldn't refuse; after all, Mama had promised Ben I would come.

Ben's family arranged for a driver to take Ben and me to Disneyland while I was there. I enjoyed spending time with Ben's family and meeting some of his friends. They had planned my visit thoughtfully, scheduling dinners and arranging for me to meet one of Ben's friends and his family at the beach. Even though Ben and I had been pen pals for over five years, I still hadn't known much about his family, and it was wonderful to spend time with them.

On my last night at their home, Ben asked me if I wanted to go see his dad at work. I said sure and later found myself on the set of TV's *Desperate Housewives*, at the time in its first season. Ben's dad was one of the show's producers, and it turned out his mom also worked in film. (She now directs the Los Angeles chapter of the Juvenile Diabetes Research Foundation.) Over the years, Ben's parents, George Perkins and Judy Ranan, have supported my work with Starlight Children's Foundation. They were with me when Starlight Children's Foundation honored Teri Hatcher from *Desperate Housewives* with the 2009 Heart of Gold Award at its gala.

When I interviewed at UCLA, I also contacted my old wish coordinator, Amy Albin. I would call her from time to time in the years following my wish. Today, Amy works at UCLA Medical Center in media relations. Her job is located in the hospital's pediatric department, and when I interviewed at UCLA for a pediatric residency position in 2004, I was able to stop by and say hello.

Finally, I emailed Kirk to tell him I was going to be in the area. He invited me to dinner at his house to meet his family. I wanted to ask Kirk about his old castmate Jeremy, but I was reluctant. I didn't know if they had kept in touch in the twelve years that had passed since *Growing Pains* had signed off. I didn't even know if Jeremy would remember meeting me all those years ago. I had lunch with the then director of Starlight that afternoon, and she urged me to ask Kirk about him that evening. "Your wish was to meet *Jeremy*! You need to ask Kirk how to get in touch with him!"

That evening at dinner Kirk's wife, Chelsea, asked me to help them find a home in New Orleans. It turned out that the whole cast of *Growing Pains* would be coming there to film a second reunion movie in a few months. I decided to hold off on my question about Jeremy, hoping I would get to see him when the cast came to New Orleans. I agreed to help them find a house to live in during filming.

CHAPTER THIRTEEN

SAYING GOODBYE TO MY FATHER

D addy died in February 2004, just three months before I graduated from Tulane.

In so many ways, Daddy and I had lived our lives out of step with each other. As a child of divorce I had learned to get by with less whenever he was concerned—less emotional support, financial assistance, pride, affection, and less of his attention—even though it was what I desired most. I had always believed that if given enough time we could eventually find our way to a healthy father-son relationship. Brenda and Jerry Glen had been successful at mending things with Daddy. Over time they had allowed themselves to find points of commonality with our father. I imagined the same would happen with me—and it almost had by the time I was preparing to graduate from Tulane.

My acceptance into the university's medical school had been a positive both for Daddy and me. But it was my second surgery between my first and second year at Tulane where the perception of change began to take hold in my family. With the additional surgery, for the first time Daddy seemed to come to terms with my need for ongoing care. Sitting in that restaurant the night before my procedure, he started to realize that I had an existing heart condition that was real—and that maybe, perhaps, the judgments he'd held against me, Mama, and Brenda were incorrect.

Unfortunately Daddy got sick shortly after that. Things reverted to the way they were before. When Daddy was diagnosed with cancer, he sat on a bench outside his doctor's office and called my brother, Jerry Glen. He told him he had likely had cancer for about ten years. His doctors had missed it continually, assuming he was suffering from back pain due to working in the oil fields. Patients with back pain of that type were usually just told to use a heating pad and take a couple of pain pills to feel better. Though prostate cancer runs in my family, Daddy didn't go to the doctor unless he absolutely had to, and never asked questions beyond the back pain recommendations. His doctor was an older small-town physician whom I had heard stories about doing double duty when he first went into practice many decades ago, working on both horses and humans. That was Jena for you.

I wanted to do what I could for him when I heard the news. Once, when he tried for two days to reach his doctor, I asked him to let me call. When I did, I left a message with his office staff saying that I was "Student-Doctor Phillips" and that I wanted to talk to him about one of his patients. The phone rang about two minutes later, and Daddy got to speak to his physician. It was something he really needed to do. A while later, I caught Daddy trying to contact his doctor saying he was Dr. Phillips. In some ways, it made me smile because I finally felt I could do something for him besides pray—which was something I had been

doing with great frequency. My emails back and forth with Kirk
Cameron were of great encouragement during this time, especially in encouraging me to pray. He had become a good friend
and a great blessing to me while I faced my dad's mortality.

He never got the opportunity to see me receive my medical
diploma. But before he died he told me he guessed I would be
going to Houston to do my residency. Then he verbally entrusted
me to Dr. Vargo, whom he believed would make sure I got what I
always wanted. It was one of the only times he didn't argue or say
anything against my future plans. Because of that conversation, I
believe he left my life knowing more about me than he ever had.
And I knew more about him.

Daddy's funeral was hard on me because I didn't feel welcome there. I did not know his side of the family very well. I grew
up around them but divorce and time had caused us to grow
apart. On the day I buried my father I needed support. Brenda
and Jerry Glen had their children and spouses. I needed Mama,
and I invited her to come with me to the ceremony, even though
Daddy's family wished I hadn't.

Some people were standoffish toward her at the wake. One
of Daddy's siblings even went as far as to directly inform Mama
that she had no right being there; another uncle told me that he
would "bounce me out of the funeral home." He hissed that the
last thing Daddy said to him was that I was ungrateful. I was
filled with anger, and it was all I could do not to tell him all the
things Daddy had told me about him. I simply walked away. I
didn't stay for Daddy's wake. I didn't feel welcomed there. The
funeral was sad and awkward; Brenda and I broke protocol to sit
in a different row, as far from Sue and her children as possible.

No one knew enough of our father-and-son story to understand where I was coming from and why I needed Mama there

with me. They didn't know about the telephone hang-ups I got whenever I would call or about all the broken promises to be there for me during my medical procedures. How I had cried on my hospital gurney because of Daddy's habit of reneging on promises. In contrast, Mama was habitually good at helping me get through hard times. I can't think of anything harder than burying your father, especially when there are so many years of hurt between you.

The funeral program listed Daddy's stepchildren ahead of his biological ones. It was hurtful to all of us. But I probably should have seen all this coming. After my maternal grandfather's funeral in 1990, Mama and I returned home to find that our outside picnic table was gone. Mama initially blamed Daddy, saying he'd seized the opportunity when he knew we were out of the house, but I didn't believe he would do that. A while later, however, I discovered while I was four-wheeler riding that the table was hidden on the backside of his property. The table was ultimately crushed by a tree during a heavy storm. Daddy never did get to enjoy that table.

There had been even more drama after my paternal grandmother's funeral. Daddy saw Mama's presence there as an invasion and was furious. He wanted me to swear I wouldn't bring Mama to his funeral, should he go first. I'd told him that was a promise I couldn't make.

Looking back, Daddy's funeral was so different from Wayne Penoli's funeral. Mama had never married him, yet he was such an integral part of our lives since he'd entered it in 1989, just after I'd made my wish. I always felt like his presence in my life was a gift from God. When he passed away unexpectedly, it was a blow. But at Wayne's funeral his ex-wife, Janine, greeted Mama, Brenda, and me very lovingly. She told us that Wayne loved each of us very much. And then she sat in the front pew throughout the ceremony holding Mama's hand.

When Daddy's graveside service ended, Mama, Brenda and her kids, and I left on our own accord. We skipped the reception to have a quiet, reflective dinner alone. It was a rough day. I had seen firsthand the effects of my father's tendency to portray himself in a better light for his family (who knows what kind of terrible things he had said about Brenda and me?) and had felt the hard slap of their anger. I was completely drained. It felt traumatic—and when it was finally over, bittersweet.

Sometime after Daddy's funeral, one of his brothers told me that my father really did love me. He just didn't understand "my world." I'd just told my uncle I'd been invited to present an award to Steven Spielberg at the Starlight Children's Foundation Gala, and he'd grown visibly uncomfortable. He told me that Daddy was a simple, hardworking man. My dreams were just way too big for him. This was probably the reason he discouraged me during my high school years. Perhaps he was just trying to keep me from getting hurt the way he may have gotten hurt by things that didn't go his way; perhaps he didn't know how much I'd be able to achieve, so he wanted to give me a reality check. I believe a lot of his actions had something to do with that.

One of my high school classmates who worked with Daddy in the oil field has told me several times that *my* dad was one of the best men that he had ever known. I wish I knew Daddy as *only* the man he knew. In fact, in the decade that has passed since my dad's death, many people have told me what a wonderful man he was. I believe Daddy was kind, generous, and loving. And I know that he did truly love me. He made a lot of mistakes, but he was my dad. I have always loved him, and I always will. There isn't a single day that passes that I do not think about him. In my own life, I strive to embody his best attributes—the ones that endeared him to many in my hometown over the course of his life. I believe it is the best way that I can honor his memory.

***

Overall, my four years at Tulane were a time of great change. Sadly, Grandma Wagoner, Mama's mama, had passed away in 2002 from complications following her 1998 open-heart surgery. The year before, Wayne, so influential in my decision to attend Tulane, died following a stroke. Although they each played such an important part in who I am today, neither they nor Daddy got the chance to see me take the biggest leap forward toward my dream yet—walking across the stage to collect my diploma.

CHAPTER FOURTEEN

CROSSING THE STAGE

G raduation at Tulane was quite a party. To our families' and friends' surprise, we all had umbrellas under our seats. In good old-fashioned New Orleans Mardi Gras tradition, once we had our diplomas in hand, we "second lined" and sashayed our way out of the auditorium led by a drum, sax, and tambourine marching trio to the sound of New Orleans street jazz.

During one of our trips to California a few years prior, Mama had encouraged Wayne to reconnect with his sister Olga. They had lost contact over the years following their mother's death. Once they reconnected they visited each other several times. Olga came to New Orleans for my graduation since Wayne could not be there to be with Mama, Brenda, and me. My good friend Matt LeBlanc's parents and sister also came. Matt could not make the ceremony because he was in the military by then and deployed overseas. Dr. Vargo and his wife, Connie, were also in attendance.

Since I didn't have a doctor in the family, Tulane agreed to let Dr. Vargo place my doctoral hood on me during the ceremony because of the role he had played in my life. He was the reason

I had decided to be a physician, so his willingness to participate in my medical school graduation truly made the day special. They had instructed us to move our tassels from one side to the other before receiving our diplomas, so that we could be "introduced properly." I'll never forget how it felt to walk up to the stage and hear "doctor" before my name for the first time. Dr. Vargo hooded me, and as we walked down the stairs together he exclaimed, "This is a great day, doctor!"

The day was bittersweet. I was sad that medical school was over, exhilarated that I had made it, and reflective of the doubts I'd had in the past. While at Tulane, Dr. Weiss, who taught clinical diagnosis class, had talked about "impostor syndrome." He described it as a medical student's feeling that the school's admissions committee made a mistake in accepting their application—that they had somehow snuck in under the radar but were not as smart as everyone else in their class.

I think all med students go through something like this. It is a panic, a feeling of secret shame, doubts about one's own worthiness and capability. I know I did—my heart surgery, the learning disability diagnosis, and my low test scores on standardized exams had plagued my mind throughout my four years there.

But my Heavenly Father had a plan. Through it all He was blessing me and putting the right people in my path as mentors and friends. It wasn't a coincidence that Kirk wrote "God bless you" on my T-shirt all those years ago. Kirk's signature was God placing His signature on my life, reminding me that He was with me every step of the way—especially during my dad's passing and all the bumps in the road that preceded it.

***

Just before my graduation, Kirk, his family, and the whole *Growing Pains* cast came to New Orleans to film.

My friend Charlotte Steger had helped me locate a beautiful historic home in New Orleans for the Camerons to rent. Kirk invited me to come to the set to watch some of the filming, which just so happened to be on location at a hospital outside of town.

I arrived on set and had to weave my way through a small crowd of people trying to get a peek at the actors with whom they had also grown up. Finally catching up to the security officer, I told him I was there to see Kirk and he pointed me in the general direction. After a few minutes of wandering around, I finally spotted him standing next to Jeremy Miller.

I paused for a second before approaching. Would Jeremy—aka "Ben Seaver"—remember me from all those years ago, from our time riding bikes all around the Warner Brothers studio lot? Had Jeremy thought about me? Had he prayed for me the way I had prayed for him?

As Kirk started to reintroduce me, Jeremy interrupted, "I know Brandon! *How are you still alive!?*"

In that moment, I knew I was not forgotten. Shocked into silence at the question, I immediately burst out laughing. Kirk and Jeremy erupted in laughter, as well, and then Jeremy gave me a big hug.

"Check it out!" he taunted Kirk, as though they were the Seaver brothers again. "Look who's back! The *one* Starlight kid who specifically requested to meet *me* on the set of *Growing Pains, not you!*" He beamed with pride, and so did I.

No longer kids looking for buildings to jump out of, Jeremy and I got together later that evening for dinner on the set. We were hoping to catch up on each other's lives, finding out where we had been and where we had plans to go. I filled him in on my journey through med school. He told me of his recent adventures before coming to New Orleans.

The way I looked at it, reconnecting would be a healing for all that I had recently been through. This fictional family had flown across the country to my neck of the woods—Louisiana. What I didn't realize yet, though, was that I wasn't the only one who needed healing. Maybe it was time *I* could be there for one of *them*. I didn't realize yet that there was much more to Jeremy's life story than I'd thought.

PART II

ANOTHER LIFE, ANOTHER WISH

CHAPTER FIFTEEN

A (SITCOM) STAR IS BORN

With my friend Jeremy's permission, I will share some of his history in this book, as his life has become so integral to mine.

Born in West Covina, California, thousands of miles from Jena, Louisiana, Jeremy Miller arrived five weeks before his due date. Like my parents, Sonja and Jim Miller had married young, with Sonja becoming an instant mom to Jim's four-year-old son, Lance. Fourteen months later, she was pregnant with Jeremy. Sonja always wanted children sooner rather than later. She got her wish and was pregnant by nineteen. The nursery was ready, Lamaze classes had been taken, but Sonja wasn't prepared for the pains of childbirth.

She was having a restless night, a nearly impossible time of falling asleep. She tossed and turned in bed, trying not to bother her husband, Jim, a sheet metal worker who had worked hard all day and was sleeping like a log. The light flickered on as she entered the bathroom at around 5:00 a.m. She was uncomfortable but not experiencing extreme pain. Still, she knew the time had come. She was in labor, and it was time to shake Jim awake.

They drove to Queen of the Valley Hospital, where her Demerol-assisted labor lasted for nearly six hours. Her doctor casually watched the Cincinnati Reds play the New York Yankees in the World Series from the waiting room, trying not to show his concern about the premature baby, as Jeremy decided when he wanted to make his big entrance. Sonja still remembers the time, 12:33 p.m. exactly, when her five-pound, fourteen-ounce, "long and skinny" nineteen-inch baby arrived. He had jaundice and was put under a fluorescent light. Nurses looked after him, giving him a bottle whenever it was time to be fed.

While Sonja was carrying Jeremy she had no idea that he'd be a boy. Her mom, Ruth Fleming, had arrived at the hospital. She wasn't allowed to come into the labor room while Sonja was in labor. Instead, she sat in the waiting room crocheting a bright red baby bunting, suitable for a baby born near the winter months and the holidays. As she was crocheting the hat, she couldn't decide if she would trim it with a cuff or ruffles. At the last moment, she decided to go with ruffles. Then, just as she finished the garment, Jim exited the labor room and excitedly declared that Jeremy was a boy. Ruth began pulling out the yarn so she could start over on the trim.

Sonja was a stay-at-home mom. She and Jim had planned for it to be that way. Jim built air-conditioning vents for a company in Baldwin Park, California. His claim to fame, even to this day, is that he worked on the air-conditioning for the Bonaventure Hotel, a famous hotel in downtown Los Angeles seen in many movies, like *This Is Spinal Tap* and *True Lies*.

Even though he already had a son, Jim was excited to have Jeremy. He was helpful with the baby, but there were limitations to the amount of time and energy he could give toward raising his son. He worked from 5:00 a.m. to 4:00 p.m., and his work was physical, dirty, and sweaty. As a result, when he came home, he was often too tired to take care of a little one. While Jim slept away the weariness, Sonja dreamed of big things for her young son. To hear her tell it, she always knew he would be a star.

Sonja was a big TV fan, especially of seventies heartthrob actor and singer Bobby Sherman. She also loved watching *The Partridge Family*. One day she took special notice of the youngest child on the show, Jeremy Gelbwaks. How could her son live a life like he was living? *Her* Jeremy was just as charming as *that* Jeremy. She flipped through a *Star* magazine to an article titled "A Day on the Set of *The Partridge Family*." The show was filmed in Burbank on what is known as the Warner Brothers Ranch. (This is the same place where *Growing Pains* would one day be filmed.) In the article, there was a picture of the cast sitting around a large table, reading scripts. Sonja zoned in on the big brown eyes of Jeremy Gelbwaks and showed the picture to her mom, Ruth. "One day, you'll have a grandson who'll do this," she predicted.

When her son was three or four months old Sonja saw an advertisement for mothers who wanted to have their baby on the cover of *Hollywood Star* magazine. It cost twenty-five dollars, which was a lot of money back then. She asked Jim if she could submit Jeremy's picture if she were able to earn it. He said yes and so the mission was on. Sonja babysat and collected cans to bring in the money. When she finally saved enough she submitted Jeremy to the contest, only to learn that it was a scam. They didn't win and neither did anybody else; it turned out that everyone who entered their baby in the competition received a mocked-up magazine with their baby on the cover—simply taped on the back.

It was the equivalent of sticking your face through the hole of the cartoon human figures at a carnival. Still, the magazine promised to send the mock-ups to agents throughout Hollywood.

If life were like a Hollywood movie, that would have been all that was needed for Jeremy to sign with an amazing, high-powered agent, land a lot of great acting jobs, and then eventually accept the role of Ben Seaver on ABC TV's *Growing Pains*. But that's not quite what happened. Years later, Sonja and Jeremy found the path to stardom, and then onto that well-known eighties television show. It was important that they did. How else would he and I have ever met? Jena is a long way from West Covina.

CHAPTER SIXTEEN

THE BIG BREAK

By the time he was six, Jeremy Miller was finally making some headway toward becoming an actor. With the help of his mother, he and his brother, Joshua, were averaging three to four auditions a day. And you think your kids have a full schedule with soccer and band practice.

Jeremy's earliest memories are of him walking around the house repeating lines from *The Brady Bunch*. He was dead on when it came to imitating the actors he saw on the small screen, which thrilled Sonja to no end. She enrolled him in singing classes around that time, where a teacher was impressed by his energetic personality and recommended that Sonja get her son into acting.

Sonja agreed. But she didn't want to push Jeremy into something he didn't want to do. She casually asked Jeremy if he wanted to be like the actors he saw on television. To a kid who was five and a half years old and was into memorizing Brady dialogue, it sounded pretty cool.

In the beginning things came easy. Jeremy was six years old

when he was cast in a McDonald's commercial where he ate cold hamburgers for six hours, trying to get the perfect take. Afterward, Sonja quit her job as a preschool teacher so she could focus on her boys. The residual checks from the Golden Arches commercial paid well, and she thought that if her sons could work, she could stay home with them and manage their careers.

Two years later, Jeremy landed a guest role on *Diff'rent Strokes*. This role was important because it offered him a chance to get a Screen Actors Guild card and be seen as an accomplished child actor. Parts on other popular shows soon followed, including *Charles in Charge*, *Pryor's Place*, and *Punky Brewster*. Then came the movie. He was cast in a full-length feature film, called *Emanon*, about a crippled child who befriends a homeless man whom he believes to be Christ. As he recalls, "It was God-awful! But I did like the process of filming something that took longer than a week to shoot."

He was seven years old at the time, and even at that age, he relished the opportunity to work on location in downtown Los Angeles. Now he was hot and booked almost everything he touched. The next movie he booked, called *Deceptions*, starred Barry Bostwick and Stefanie Powers, and required Jeremy and his family to travel to London for filming.

Although the second movie was much better, Jeremy's early jobs didn't prove he was a great actor destined for stardom—just that he was a serviceable child actor, capable of showing up on a movie, television, or commercial set, ready and willing to do the work. But they gave Sonja the faith to believe that what her son was pursuing was more than just a pipe dream.

That faith served her well when, between the ages of seven and eight, Jeremy's job offers began to dry up. Sonja and Jim had divorced when Jeremy was two years old and Josh was just an infant, and Jim had gotten the house in the settlement. He'd remarried and moved his new wife and kids into the house. That left Sonja and her two boys with only the option of moving in with her family in Alhambra—with her mom and dad, and, for a while, her brother and sister, too.

Jeremy loved living with his grandparents even though he had to share a room with Sonja and his brother. "It was heaven," Jeremy recalls. "I spent my free time growing up shooting pool and playing poker. It was all good, wholesome stuff. The tough part was traveling eighty miles round trip to Hollywood and Venice, California, where most of my auditions were held."

Sonja believed in Jeremy and Joshua, but the commute and time became an issue, especially because they didn't have much to show for it. She wasn't sure how much more energy she could invest in the long drives. Jeremy spent his days doing homework in the backseat of a car while Sonja drove him and Joshua from one audition to the next. But he felt no anxiety because he had Sonja's strength to rely on. He was also content spending time with his mom and brother. They went to auditions and sat in casting rooms with other child actors whom he would come to know very well. Young actors like Jaleel White, R. J. Williams, and Brandon Call were Jeremy's acting companions who would eventually go on to make names for themselves, as well, featured on such ABC shows as *Family Matters*, *Full House*, and *Step by Step*.

After about three hundred auditions and a handful of guest shots on prime-time series, Jeremy finally got "the call" from his agent asking him to head out to Warner Brothers in Burbank and try out for the role of Ben Seaver. Thanks to the success of NBC's *The Cosby Show* and *Family Ties*, ABC was looking for its own family sitcom hit and had a lot riding on *Growing Pains*.

Early in the day Jeremy was ushered into a room where he sat across from the show's producers, writers, and director. Plucked out of three hundred hopeful kids, he said he doesn't remember reading lines from a script. Instead, he told stories, jokes, and did his best dolphin impressions. He often would place a rubber snake under the casting agent's table as a practical joke! Looking back, Jeremy believed it wasn't talent they were seeking. What mattered most was a kid with personality. They were looking to cast cute precociousness. "I have nothing but fun memories," he recalls. "But today, when I give advice to parents interested in seeing their children become actors and actresses, I find myself telling them to make sure their child really wants to do it. I have seen firsthand how some kids were forced into the process. Sadly, their moms and dads were more enthused about stardom than they were."

Jeremy would be the first to say he didn't get to have a normal childhood, but he believes the trade-off far outweighs what he missed.

Jeremy's agent had a habit of ringing a bell whenever a client booked a part. So, true to form, when he got the part of Ben Seaver, the bell was rung. The family celebrated by going to the local Dairy Queen for banana splits. But while they were there, they had something very important to discuss. Jeremy had also been offered a role on a television series called *Fathers and Sons*, starring Merlin Olsen. As they say, when it rains it pours.

At the time *Fathers and Sons*, a sitcom about a father who coaches his son's baseball team, was being produced by 20th Century Fox Television for NBC, which was ruling in the ratings race. It was hard to choose something outside NBC, but Jeremy's mother and grandmother had an instinct. They had faith in the premise of *Growing Pains*, so they signed contracts with ABC before Jeremy had even performed his final screen test. (Thank goodness for a mother's intuition: *Fathers and Sons* premiered on April 6, 1986, and was canceled by the network on May 4 that same year after just four episodes due to poor ratings.)

The *Growing Pains* screen test felt very familiar to Jeremy. He had done guest spots on television shows before. Initially it seemed to be pretty much the same. The reality was, however, that Jeremy had been cast in a project that was destined to go on for a very long time. Before he got *Growing Pains*, Jeremy never knew acting could be a career. He had earned some money through acting, sure, but he'd been raised in a pretty ordinary family—blue collar and normal.

The first day on set, Jeremy was introduced to Kirk Cameron, his older TV brother Mike. He later met Tracey Gold, who would play Carol Seaver. Jeremy's first impressions of his television siblings were good. He immediately saw that Kirk was a fun guy. Like his character, Jeremy related to him as if he were an older brother and someone from whom he could learn a lot. Jeremy fondly recalled the relationship he built with Kirk and Tracey during their on-set school hours, playing pranks when they should have been studying. They'd soap up the schoolroom trailer windows, pass notes, crack jokes, and make prank phone calls pretending to be calling from the set and summoning each other back to work. It helped offset the weekly grind and stress of filming television.

Jeremy's favorite episode was the time the entire cast got to go to Hawaii for a special two-part episode. Another favorite had Ben and Mike driving around locations in L.A. at night, looking for glue. Hanging out with Kirk, for Jeremy, was almost too much fun to be considered work.

He wasn't aware of how successful the show had become with the American public. ABC had originally bought thirteen episodes. Before the season ended, the network asked for nine more *Growing Pains* episodes to be filmed. That's when Jeremy started to realize that the show was liked—really liked. He was making $2,500 per episode—not a bad salary for an eight-year-old.

If only his real life were as neat and tidy as his fictional one.

CHAPTER SEVENTEEN

THE MERGING OF FAMILIES

When Jeremy's dad left the family, he moved into an apartment not too far from the family home. Though he was out of the house the living arrangement enabled Jim to see his young sons every other weekend. It was important for him to remain involved in both Jeremy's and Joshua's lives by being present for all of their school and sporting events. The reason for this could have been the direct result of his experience with his oldest son, Lance.

Lance was four years old when Jeremy was born and six when Joshua arrived. From the beginning, Sonja loved Lance as if he were her own. She wanted nothing more than for him to be an ongoing part of her new life with Jim. She'd even made plans for him to be the ring bearer in their wedding. But a week before the marriage, Lance's mom left with the child and he could not be found. It was devastating for both Sonja and Jim, who married without him present and then immediately took action to find him. They did not see him again until nine months later, when his mom finally returned from Texas with him. The months of separation were costly for the Miller family. They had invested a lot of time and money into finding Jim's son. Eventually, a court ruling would ensure that Lance wouldn't be taken away again. One can only speculate that perhaps that's why Jim clung to his kids well after his marriage ended with Sonja.

However, trouble arose when Sonja set her sights on having more children. Jim enjoyed his kids but, Jeremy believes, was growing restless with the idea of playing father to more little ones and appeared jealous of the amount of attention Sonja gave her boys, Lance included.

Keeping up with his kids after the divorce meant Jim would meet Sonja at gas stations or McDonald's restaurant parking lots for the custody exchanges. Life was stable until Jeremy turned six and his dad, now remarried, decided that he needed the house Sonja and the boys were living in for his new wife and kids. After the loss of the family home, Sonja and the boys moved to Alhambra, where life was downsized to just one bedroom for the trio. Jeremy enjoyed the closeness of having his mom, brother, aunt, uncle, Cousin Briana, and Grampa Jim, who was a veteran and close family friend who lived with his grandparents, all staying under one roof. Grandma Ruth was happy to have everyone at her home; she loved having her grandbabies on her lap at the end of a workday.

Jim continued to see the boys every other weekend; they had a very traditional 1980s-style custody arrangement. He would sometimes come by to see the kids during the week if something special was going on, attending Jeremy's little league games even if he had to leave work early. After the game, Jim would make up the time he'd missed by returning to his job and working into the night.

Jeremy doesn't remember arguments or fights between his

parents, and he remembers being close with his father. To his knowledge, Sonja and Jim tried to create an amicable situation, especially when they were in the presence of their children. And yet, as with any divorce, the separation was hard on everyone. Sonja was devastated. As a child Jeremy assumed that since it was his dad who left, he must have been okay with it, but nothing could have been further from the truth. Years later Jeremy would discover that Jim often felt like a failure for not being able to work things out. Jeremy attributes the breakup to immaturity: "I think my parents married too young. Dad wasn't prepared for children or marriage. He found himself having to be too responsible too soon." Jim couldn't be totally present because he was on the typical working man's treadmill—wake up, go to work, come home, eat dinner, sit in front of the TV for a bit, go to bed, and then wake up to do it all over again. It was up to Sonja to deal with the kids. In the end it was easier to give up on the marriage than to try to work things out. It required less energy.

Four years after the divorce, Jim met Carol. The two started dating when Jeremy was six. When he and Carol married and, subsequently, moved into the West Covina home, Jeremy got a stepmom and two stepbrothers. Now every other weekend hanging out with his dad meant spending time with his brothers—all of them. Jim worked the schedule out to where Jeremy, Joshua, and Lance were all at the house on the same weekends.

Jeremy loved the time he got to spend with his brothers during those summer days; they kept themselves entertained by playing football in the park. Lance was very good at being the older brother and planning things for them to do. Today, Jeremy told me, he gets along very well with Carol and his stepbrother, Ryan, but at the time, like many kids of divorce, he found it difficult to always take a backseat to the others.

Jeremy always felt his father was supportive of his acting career. Jim never offered to pitch in with gas or rides, but he was regular with alimony and child-support payments. Even when Jeremy was doing the show and making good money, Jim kept up with his child-support payments. Overall, Jeremy's dad thought his job on *Growing Pains* was cool, even though he didn't come to the television set often. Jeremy wished he would.

The time Jeremy spent with his dad was very special. When they both had time off from work, Jim would sometimes take Jeremy and Joshua away for the weekend. They'd check into a hotel, see movies, go to the park, and just have fun. Those were great times for Jeremy. Jeremy fondly remembers when his dad accompanied him on a charter bus on an ABC Television publicity trip. They headed down to the San Diego Zoo with other teen celebrities and their parents. They had a great time, but Jim was so blue collar, he always kept his son grounded. (He wasn't impressed with, as he called it, "all the glitz and crud.") That weekend, they saw other child actors being rude to their parents and misbehaving. Jim made it very clear that such behavior was not acceptable from him.

Jeremy also credits his dad for his faith in God. His dad was a born-again Christian and attended a megachurch. Jeremy attended with his dad every other weekend. Jim influenced his faith in many ways. Over time, Jeremy watched him grow in what he believed. And though he didn't always agree with Jim's interpretation of certain parts of Christianity, Jeremy felt he came to resemble the most important attributes of Christ—love and forgiveness—which are some of the same traits he would later see in his friend Kirk Cameron.

Over the years, the biggest struggle between Jeremy and Jim has been the amount of time they have been able to spend together. There were things that Jeremy could have and should have shared with his dad. Jim was a busy man, and he had a new life with an additional family whose care was his responsibility. Jeremy still wishes there could have been more time together, and he's confident his father would say the same thing.

CHAPTER EIGHTEEN

PRIVATE LIFE, PUBLIC PERSON

Sadly, as we know, child stars often deal with fallout from taking on a career at such a young age. During his *Growing Pains* years, Jeremy was synonymous with the character he played—a precocious little kid famous for delivering the "Ben Seaver Scream." I, along with the millions of others who watched the highly-rated television show, got a real kick out of hearing the high-pitched sound Ben Seaver made whenever he found himself in a situation he couldn't handle. It endeared him to us, his fans. It made me want to be his friend. I was caught up in the sitcom's "laughter and love," because my own world seemed way too serious.

But sadly, there were parts of Jeremy's off-screen life that contrasted with his show's easygoing storylines. Jeremy is a child of divorce. Although I had assumed his showbiz childhood was all glitter and fun, we experienced many of the same emotional things that arise from being the product of a broken home.

While I got through by focusing on my health and education, Jeremy focused on his acting career and learning to cultivate a persona. Unlike the character he portrayed on television, his responsibilities included growing up in a household where he was the oldest of four boys, sustaining an adult-size living at the age of eight that his family came to depend on, and relating to a world filled with adults who often expected him to act less like a child and more like a professional.

Fortunately he had Alan Thicke and Kirk Cameron to admire. Tracey Gold was also someone he learned to confide in throughout the run of the show. To this day his connection with his television family remains, as does the specific respect Jeremy holds for Kirk. Jeremy still sees Kirk as an older brother role model to be admired for his faith in God. Jeremy won't hesitate to say that he's grateful they came into each other's life.

Jeremy's stepfather came into his life when he was eleven years old. In the spring of 1987, Jeremy was performing in a musical group in Orange County, California, at Knott's Berry Farm for ABC Television. His future stepfather was involved in the production, which included four weeks of rehearsals and two weeks of performances. "My first impression of him was that he was this big kid. I remember instantly having good feelings toward him because he seemed like a great guy and was fun to be around," Jeremy recalled.

Once Jeremy started to get to know the man who would become his stepfather, he encouraged his mom to get to know him, too. When the musical show ended, Sonja started to date him, which pleased little matchmaker Jeremy. It wasn't long before both he and his brother, Josh, began to ask probing questions about their relationship. The boys wanted to know when the two were going to get married. In their own way they pushed the issue in the hopes that this "real nice guy" would become a permanent fixture in their lives.

On October 18, 1988, Sonja married Jeremy's stepfather in the main ballroom at the Universal Sheraton Hotel. Kirk, Tracey, and other *Growing Pains* cast members attended the ceremony. He had asked Jeremy to be his best man; Sonja asked Jeremy to call him "Dad." Jeremy agreed to both.

In the beginning, he seemed like the missing part of the Miller household. He seemed to love Sonja deeply and genuinely care for her children. Even before they'd wed, he would invite Jeremy and Josh to his house to watch movies when Sonja wasn't around so they could get to know each other. His male influence on the boys was not lost on Sonja. She welcomed it as much as she welcomed their relationship; there was a palpable sense of relief in having him join the family.

From the outside looking in, the life of an actor appears to be a dream. With all the money, fortune, and fame, we tend to put the people we see on the small and big screen on a pedestal, longing to have the lives we imagine they have. Before the days of stalker paparazzi and *TMZ*, showing us the way our current stars eat a sandwich or parallel park, we used to only see the glamorous side of celebrity life. In the eighties, we just had the Life section of *USA Today* and John Tesh and Mary Hart interviews, giving us the highly manipulated, publicist-controlled glimpses of the rich and famous.

There was Jeremy Miller in the teen magazines, posing in brightly colored Ocean Pacific clothes. There he was on *Growing Pains*, getting laughs from several hundred people. There he was on *Entertainment Tonight*, talking about his latest charity event—to a captive adult reporter who seemed to hang on every word. Why? Because he was a star!

As a young boy, I coveted the character he portrayed. My Starlight Children's Foundation wish was really made so I could meet my hero, Ben Seaver. His character lived out what I wanted. And the character placed Jeremy in an enviable position, too; it gave him the opportunity to experience a life that many would never have. Though I didn't know Jeremy at the time, I celebrated that for him.

It wasn't long after his stepfather moved into the Miller home that Jeremy's behavior began to change. "I came to realize that he was jealous of my success and the fact that I made a bit more money," Jeremy told me later. "By the time he came into our lives at that Knott's Berry Farm show, I had been steadily working for three years in television. When we met, the family was already pretty comfortable financially."

When not running a sound board, Jeremy's stepfather made his living in advertising. Once he and Sonja married, he began working as a publicist, promoting celebrities. Jeremy was his first client, and he received 5 percent of everything Jeremy earned. Besides deciding what Jeremy would do in his public life, he handled press relations for a few other young actors, as well, and did some advertising on the side. Both efforts didn't bring in enough to support the kind of lifestyle he wanted the family to have.

He bought, tore down, and then rebuilt a gigantic house for his family. He then filled it with $3,000 pinball machines, a $10,000 stereo system, and a number of new cars. The money he made representing Jeremy, plus as much of Jeremy's cut as the Coogan Law (the child actor's trust law) would allow, was being spent very quickly. He began advising Jeremy to turn down parts if he felt they didn't pay enough. In Jeremy's view, he often made business decisions that overlooked what the rest of the family, particularly Jeremy, wanted.

"There was a time when I believed investing in a Taco Bell restaurant near Warner Brothers Studios would be a great financial idea," Jeremy recalled of a business venture that he was forced to turn down. "Unfortunately, he did not see it that way. Today, that same Taco Bell is still going strong as an off-site studio staple. Though no one can predict the future, I was made to believe that I had no business acumen, and therefore whatever I said wasn't worth considering." Although Jeremy's business accounts provided 90 percent of the family's income, his opinion was often given minimal consideration.

Sonja wanted to trust in her husband's decisions. On the other hand, Jeremy was her son. Sonja never stopped making him and her other kids the main priority. In Jeremy's view, his stepfather interpreted her defenses of Jeremy as a sign that she loved her kids more than she did him, and he responded by becoming a bully seemingly bent on destroying the confidence he saw in Jeremy.

Even if his acting career hadn't been a consideration, Jeremy's status as the oldest son of a single mother made him a target for someone struggling to assume the position as the head of a household. One night, a family screaming match occurred when he became upset after Sonja served Jeremy his dinner plate first. The argument ended with him throwing the food onto the floor.

Jeremy and Sonja had a strong bond that he couldn't break. Still, Jeremy increasingly perceived that he tried to set a wedge between them and began putting Jeremy in his place in ways that could be less than tenderhearted.

Years later, Jeremy would tell Sonja and his dad, Jim, about the way his stepfather had treated him when they traveled together. He had kept that hidden from everyone—everyone except Tracey Gold and one therapist. Jeremy and I have made the decision not to share the details even though they affected his emotional well-being.

As a result of his experiences, Jeremy began to experience social anxiety at the age of twelve. His personality transformed. He was no longer the outgoing kid who liked to entertain; he started turning inward and pulling away from people and situations. His stepfather's presence in the house became a dark force for Jeremy—one that made him pull inward. His confidence faltered.

By the age of fourteen, Jeremy was ready to tell his stepfather enough was enough. He'd gained confidence through karate classes and had physically come into his body. He was no longer willing to take everything his stepfather was dishing out. He recalled: "I remember the night he and Josh had an argument on opposite sides of the room that ended with him charging at Josh. I jumped over the stair rail, positioning myself between the two of them. I told him that in order to get to Josh he'd have to go through me first. Fortunately, just the thought of that made him back down."

Sonja ended the marriage some time later. By the time things ended, there wasn't a whole lot of love left in their relationship. But the consequences still showed themselves in Jeremy's behavior.

He had lost almost all confidence when it came to attending events or being in public; he began habitually throwing up on the *Growing Pains* set before taping nights. At the age of twelve, Jeremy recalls being invited to a volleyball party in Manhattan Beach, California. Alcohol was readily accessible there.

His only other exposure to liquor had occurred while cleaning up after his grandparents' parties. As a curious child, Jeremy would finish off the last swallow or two in a can of beer left out. That had gone on for a year or two, until he'd come across a can that someone had used as an ashtray—and that was the last time he did that. This experience was different. The alcohol seemed to numb his pain; for the first time in a long time, he felt fun, social, free. He drank an entire case of beer by himself. It was on this trip that he realized he didn't have an off switch.

When *Growing Pains* ended, Jeremy was fifteen. On top of the level of anxiety brought on by his relationship with his step-father, he now found himself going through teenage angst. The combination of both emotional states made for a difficult situation. He wanted to feel normal; he wanted to live the life other teenagers did. He began to pursue girls and go to parties rather than spending weekends with his father.

It wasn't long before a pre-party drink became a part of his routine for going out. Once he was at the party, he had quite a few more. Though he kept it to himself, there were times he wondered if others knew. He would sneak away to the bathroom to drink from a flask while at a family dinner, or sneak away to drink in his car during lunch breaks on set. *Wasn't it obvious?* he'd wonder.

Jeremy was around seventeen years old when his dad began treating him like an adult. During one of their once-a-month dinners, Jim decided to have a serious talk with his son. Jim pointedly spoke to Jeremy about drinking and partying. He wanted him to know that if he drank, he should call him. There would be no judgment, no punishment; Jim would come and get him. It was clear that Jeremy's dad worried about his son drinking and driving or getting into a car with someone who was intoxicated. Jeremy knew his dad to be a strict Christian, having certain boundaries in his own life. The conversation they shared that night meant a lot to Jeremy, who believed it was the first time Jim dropped the "dad cloak" and related to him as a human being.

Addiction runs in Jeremy's family. His paternal grandfather

had his own issues with alcohol when he was younger. And though Jim had decided not to drink, he had some awareness of what it meant to be around an addictive personality. He knew Jeremy drank, and he worried for his son but he did not know the extent of his alcohol issues. Jeremy was just too good at maintaining the appearance of normalcy around his dad even while drinking. For the most part Jeremy knew how to hold it together in front of family, friends, and even coworkers. He only let loose when he was alone or in the company of people to whom it didn't matter.

He'd always wanted to impress his father, which is why he did his best to hide it from him. He also hid it because drinking made him feel better. Drinking was like having a shield; it loosened up his social anxiety, boosted his confidence, and gave him a slight edge that no one knew about. Keeping it a secret meant he could hold on to that edge for longer.

Jeremy started having real problems with addiction around the age of nineteen. He began smoking marijuana regularly in college, and then alcohol took precedence again. He didn't seem to have an off button; once he got going, he lacked the ability to say when he'd had enough. On an *Oprah* episode in 2016, Jeremy recalled of his college years: "There were times when I was so filled with self-loathing and self-hatred, and then combine that with the alcohol and the lack of judgment that provides... It's a very good thing that I never owned a gun because I don't know what would have happened. ... And that's scary."

It took a while for him to graduate from beer to hard alcohol. He couldn't seem to keep mixed drinks down until his tolerance grew, and one day he found he could drink as much as he wanted. The drinking helped soothe the social anxiety disorder he had been dealing with since his stepfather had come into his life. The addiction had its purpose.

CHAPTER NINETEEN

THE PHONE STOPS RINGING

The University of Southern California was the "it" college for film and television studies. It boasts such notable alumni as Ron Howard and George Lucas. But it was not a good match for Jeremy. As he told me, "I really wish my college experience had been better, but it was a little bit of my own doing—or undoing—at first. I just didn't realize what a valuable experience it was and how much I could really get out of it."

Having been in show business since he was a child, there wasn't a whole lot he could relate to in the theater program during his first year of classes. In his freshman year, the emphasis was on stage movement. It was interesting, but as an actor used to the grind and speed of network television, Jeremy didn't feel like he was getting much out of it. Of course, college demands a period of adjustment; he had planned for that. What he didn't foresee was his breaking his ankle at a tennis tournament just months into his first semester.

The break forced him to drop three of his classes because they involved movement. Shortly after he came down with mononucleosis and had to withdraw from the semester completely. For the first year of school he was either sick or smoking pot in his room. His college experience was entirely different from my own. I blossomed and came out of my shell, but two-thousand-plus miles away Jeremy was retreating.

Jeremy never went back to USC. This was partly because of his health circumstances and also because of finances. His choice of college was not cheap. To pay tuition Jeremy had had to dip into what was left of his *Growing Pains* savings. Paying for a four-year education would deplete all he had, leaving him nothing to fall back on. He decided to return to his acting career and to spend his money on private coaching, which seemed far more cost-effective.

But getting back into acting was hard. Jeremy got a few auditions and a few callbacks, but nothing ever panned out. Hollywood had become impenetrable to the once-famous child star. Things had been easier when his mom and brother were by his side, championing his auditions and supporting his career with their encouragement. Now he was among the shuffled deck of struggling actors. According the Screen Actors Guild, only about 15 percent of all actors in Hollywood are employed. Jeremy had had a long run on a popular sitcom but he couldn't find any work at all. Things were falling apart.

At first Jeremy blamed his representation for not pushing him hard enough for roles for which he believed he was a perfect fit. But when he traded his agent and agency for a manager who seemed to be working harder for him, he didn't fare any better. His few opportunities seemed to be on low-budget productions—independent films and small television roles. He realized that taking time off from the industry had been a mistake. With no idea how to reestablish himself, he finally chose to go in a different direction.

At the age of twenty-three, he decided to go to culinary school. It was something that had been on his mind for a long time. He'd gotten the bug back when he worked for his grandparents in their restaurant during his hiatus from *Growing Pains*. Jeremy applied for some loans and enrolled in an eighteen-month cooking program at the famed Le Cordon Bleu College of Culinary Arts in Pasadena, California.

Le Cordon Bleu wasn't college, but this was the most fun he'd had learning anything in his life. He even liked the math classes that focused on the scientific aspects of preparing food. (A love of math is something I didn't know Jeremy and I held in common until writing this book.)

In some ways, Jeremy's life problems had a lot to do with what he could and couldn't let go. We had long since lost contact, as he had with many other friends. He began hanging out solely with new friends he'd met at parties; he didn't want those who knew him best, like his family or Kirk, to see what a mess he was becoming. He had also chosen to step away from the church. Over time he'd grown disappointed with organized religion. He believed in God but the seemingly arbitrary rules of the church drove him away. Finally he began to run from his faith in God, as well. He felt as though he was hiding from God—running, yet again, from someone he didn't want to let down. And now he had left acting—the career that had given his life so much meaning.

The one thing he couldn't let go was alcohol. For the most part, the control it had over him remained a secret. He was one of those guys who carried a flask. He got his work done throughout culinary school. He hid his drinking and maintained a successful appearance in class. He kept ugly episodes to a minimum. He was a happy drunk. Until he wasn't.

After a few years, he began to black out and act up. He

eventually became an angry alcoholic, unconcerned about drinking in the open. He began to feel that everyone knew anyway; he no longer cared what anyone thought.

In 2000, at the age of twenty-four, Jeremy was asked to take a leave of absence from culinary school to head to Montreal and film *The Growing Pains Movie*, the first TV reunion for the show. Jeremy agreed, believing he would make it back to culinary school once production wrapped on the film.

The movie was very special to Jeremy because it meant reconnecting with the whole cast. They had all run into each other at different times over the years, but this was the first time they were under one roof for an extended period of time. "It was like the whole family was back together again," Jeremy recalled.

For the most part, filming the first *Growing Pains* movie went well. It seemed being back with the cast made him want to keep things under control. He would drink only at night, waking with a raging hangover and working hard through the day before doing it all over again. He avoided drinking on set or at lunch, so he thought he was hiding it well enough. But some of his fellow cast members took note of the odd behavior. They wondered just what was going on with Ben Seaver.

Jeremy never finished culinary school. His mother and his family needed help financially and Jeremy felt it was best for him to begin earning money. He skipped his last section and externship to pursue auditions and cooking jobs. That decision led to him failing the program. Without school to go back to Jeremy began looking for a real job. He found that restaurants weren't paying as much as he would have liked, and it was very difficult to get a job as a recognizable actor. Hiring managers assumed he would walk away as soon as he got an audition. After doing the math he realized there was more money in catering. The money he would have spent on tuition was something he could give to help care for his mom and brothers.

Family was, and is, everything to Jeremy. Sonja had sacrificed so much to make sure he realized his dream of acting that this felt like the least he could do. All of those long drives to auditions, to the stage of the sitcom for rehearsal days, to the late nights of taping in front of a live audience—Sonja had been there the whole way, giving and giving to her son. Jeremy didn't regret helping his mother, nor did he regret having to leave USC and then later Le Cordon Bleu. The only thing he would have done differently was immerse himself more into the work. He would have tried to experience college life as a whole, not just the parties. To this day, he imagines all the wonderful stories he would have been able to tell about his college days.

Jeremy's catering jobs found him working special events around town. He was being requested personally by groups large and small, and even some companies. He not only made and served food but he also successfully transitioned into teaching cooking classes for private groups. It was a lot of fun. It was a way for him to express himself creatively while distracting him from a town that had stopped calling. Or so he thought.

He'd finally gotten the call for the sitcom's second reunion movie, *Growing Pains: Return of the Seavers*, to be filmed in Louisiana. Hollywood had finally reached out, and it brought Jeremy back to me.

PART III

THE CIRCLE COMPLETED

CHAPTER TWENTY

LOSING AND GAINING FAMILY MEMBERS

D uring the rest of the time *Growing Pains* was in town, I continued to hang around the set. In fact, I began to stop by most every day. Joanna Kerns, who was both acting in and directing the movie, said I was more than welcome to be there.

I was scheduled for a clinical rotation that month that would have been quite time consuming, but Tulane allowed me to change my schedule to a computers in medicine class for the month so my load would be lighter. It met only once or twice a week for an hour. They knew my father had just passed away and they were very accommodating to my emotional state of mind.

Kirk began to call me more often to pick him up to run errands or pick Chelsea and the kids up at the airport whenever they flew in. A few times he called to ask for directions. Since my apartment was only a few minutes away, I usually offered just to take him where he was going. It was a blessing to have Kirk and his family in town to help occupy my time after Daddy's death.

One of my favorite memories from my month with the *Growing Pains* cast was talking over residency options with Tracey Gold and Alan Thicke. Tracey's vote was for me to go to Mayo Clinic for residency. While I didn't go there for my pediatrics residency, I did go there for my pediatric cardiology fellowship. I talked with Alan about how he had once been interested in going to medical school and relayed to the cast my crazy stories of life in the Big Easy.

Kirk and I continued to hang out when he wasn't working and when his family was in California. We went to the gym at Tulane, and the student worker at the front desk did not believe him when she asked his name to add to the guest log until he showed her his identification. He went to church with me one Sunday. He introduced me to raw sushi, something I'd avoided up until that point because of the chewy texture. (It was odd at first, but eventually I did find some rolls I liked—although Kirk seemed convinced that I hated it all and was just humoring him.) We talked about anything and everything and continued to build a strong friendship.

When Chelsea and the kids were in town and Kirk was filming, about two weeks after my father's funeral, we went to the Audubon Zoo in New Orleans. While there, we went to watch the elephants perform around noon. I had Kirk's middle son on my shoulders so he could see better. Coincidentally, we ran into Daddy's wife Sue and her family. I had been watching the elephants for a few minutes before I even realized that she was standing right next to me. New Orleans is a four-hour drive from Jena, and I'd had no idea they would be in town. I was struck with surprise that we had ended up at exactly the same place at exactly the same time.

After we moved on from the elephants' show, Chelsea could

sense that I was uneasy. When I explained what had happened, she told me, "I am glad you are here with us," to reassure me. I realized God was telling me something with this coincidence. I shouldn't let the hurt that I had felt throughout my childhood consume me. God was letting me know that He understood the real intention of my childhood wish: to have a family who cared about me, blood-related or not.

Reestablishing a friendship with Jeremy was slower going. I felt that he was on the fence about trusting me. There seemed to be some distance between us, but I wasn't sure why. I attributed it to all the time that had passed since I'd seen him last.

We occasionally had dinner together in the French Quarter near his hotel. One Saturday evening Jeremy, my friend Nick Darby, and I stayed out all night exploring the French Quarter until everything shut down around 7:30 a.m. Sunday morning. I should have suspected that Jeremy had a problem with alcohol because he almost always had a drink in his hand, but I thought he was just enjoying New Orleans. From that time on, Jeremy and I stayed in touch. I knew how to contact him, and I felt at ease doing so.

The last day of filming the reunion movie also happened to be on Match Day, when I was to find out where I was doing my residency. Jeremy was supposed to go with me, but at the last minute, his shooting schedule changed. I had stayed with him at the Iberville Suites Hotel in an extra guest room the night before, but the following morning he received his call sheets, giving him an earlier call time. I said goodbye and went downstairs to have breakfast. I ran into Nancy Johnson, whose daughter Ashley played Chrissy Seaver. Nancy offered to come with me.

Nancy and I made our way over to the ballroom of the hotel where the ceremony was held. Dr. Marc Kahn, who was the associate dean for student affairs, started the festivities by playing his trumpet, a Tulane Medical School tradition. The trumpet performance was followed by students being called forward to receive an envelope containing their future. Some of them ran up to the front of the room. I was one of the last students to be called; I watched the faces of those around me and their spouses and guests. A few looked disappointed, while others lit up with excitement. I tried to steel myself for potential disappointment. But when I tore into my envelope, it said "Baylor College of Medicine." I would spend the next three years of my medical education with Dr. Vargo at Texas Children's Hospital!

Later that day I filled everyone in on what had happened while having lunch on set with Kirk and Jeremy. While we were eating, to my surprise, Dr. Vargo called to congratulate me and let me know that he would be serving as my academic advisor during my time at Texas Children's Hospital. It seemed like everything was coming together; my childhood dream had come to fruition.

As I took in the moment, it occurred to me that this day was linked in a very special way to the day I had first met Jeremy and Kirk on the set of *Growing Pains* fifteen years earlier. After all, I didn't start to do exceptionally well in school until after my Starlight wish. That was the first year I made all A's. I had continued to do so from then until I graduated from Louisiana Tech. God seemed to be putting His signature on my accomplishments, reminding me that they were not mine alone and that He had been with me every step of the way. I thought back to the dream I'd had about the *Growing Pains* cast being with me on the day of my white coat ceremony, back at the start of medical school. Who would have thought I'd be with them now, all these years later, on another day that was so important to my future?

I ended Match Day at the *Growing Pains* wrap party. It was the last day of shooting and the last time everyone would be together. It was there that I met Orion Griffiths. Orion was a teenage street-performing acrobat who was a member of a traveling family circus. Actress Ashley Johnson, Nancy's daughter, had befriended him after watching him perform near Jackson Square in the French Quarter. At the time I had no way of knowing that I would run across Orion performing on the streets of San Francisco six years later, or that Mama and I would eventually travel to New York City to see him perform as an acrobat in Broadway's *Pippen*. Again, family and that sense of connectivity were all around me. I couldn't imagine a better time to receive and embrace it.

When the actors left New Orleans, I wondered if I would ever see Kirk and Jeremy again. I was alone in the city once more. It was quiet, literally and emotionally. There was time to think about Daddy and to feel the fresh pain of having lost him all over again. Until two weeks later—the phone rang. Kirk was on the other end, calling just to check on me.

That's what family does, especially this new one that God had given me. They may have been a fictional family to a large TV audience, but for me, they had become a real-life extension of my own.

CHAPTER TWENTY-ONE

THE STRUGGLE OF ADDICTION

I didn't know the seriousness of the alcohol problem that Jeremy was struggling with during his time on the set of *Return of the Seavers*. After showing up late for the movie's initial table read with the cast and crew, Jeremy made it through the first two weeks okay. He couldn't be on the set without some type of alcohol in his hand. He was a "functioning drinker" who was dealing fairly well with call times, memorizing character lines, and trying to present a sense of normalcy to people who had known him since he was a child. What wasn't normal were the feelings that began to stir inside him—the same ones associated with his thoughts about his relationship with his stepfather. They seemed to surface uncontrollably, upsetting him, no matter how hard he tried to work through them or force them away with alcohol. There is no doubt he needed someone to talk to about his insecurities; however, I couldn't be that person. We had just reintroduced ourselves and were getting to know each other again.

One evening, after an eighteen-hour day on set, Jeremy took the elevator up to his room. He was bone tired, wanting nothing more than to change into his swimsuit and sit in the hot tub with a stiff drink before turning in for the night.

Joanie, another guest at the hotel, entered the elevator with some of her family. They were headed out in search of food. In screenplays, this chance encounter is what writers refer to as the "meet-cute"—when two people bump into each other. "Do you know where we can find the Burger King near here?" Joanie asked Jeremy.

He told them he didn't think it was open but gave them directions to it anyway. He also gave them a backup option.

"You know who you look like?" Joanie asked.

"No."

"The kid from *Growing Pains*," she insisted.

"I've heard that a lot over the years," Jeremy said with a smirk. "It's probably...because I *am* that kid."

She laughed and smacked him on the arm. "No, you aren't. Shut up."

Jeremy explained that the cast was in New Orleans shooting a reunion movie. He got off the elevator, made his way to his room, poured himself a drink, changed his clothes, and headed back to the elevator. Once again, he ran into the women. They had just returned with their fast food.

He went on to say that he didn't know anyone there other than the cast, so it would be nice if the two of them could grab dinner, go to a club, or just go out and have fun while he was in town. He gave them his room number.

The next morning Joanie slipped a note under Jeremy's door, mentioning how nice it was to meet him. She asked for an autographed script in the note, ending it by giving him her room number. When Jeremy called Joanie, she let him know she'd be downstairs at the pool with her friends. Jeremy didn't have to be on set so he was able to spend the whole day at the pool with Joanie. Jeremy found Alan Thicke and Tracey Gold at the pool, too, but things reached a point between Joanie and him that it felt like it was just the two of them, sitting and talking, getting to know one another.

They had an instant connection. After everyone left, including his TV father and TV sister, Jeremy and Joanie stayed in the pool for four more hours. Finally hungry, they went to dinner together. They ended the night at a jazz club in the hotel with Joanie's family. It was Mardi Gras in New Orleans, so they hung out and drank the night away.

Jeremy eventually left Joanie an autographed script for her at the hotel's front desk. He also invited her back to New Orleans, three or four times, to hang out before production on the movie ended.

The two ended up dating, long distance, for several years. (They were grateful for their unlimited friends and family plan, because they averaged more than 10,000 minutes a month on their cell phones!) They also traveled back and forth to see each other every few months—Joanie flying to Los Angeles or Jeremy visiting Corpus Christi, Texas.

Joanie had three little boys, aged five, nine, and twelve. Jeremy had first been introduced to the kids back in Corpus Christi at the Texas State Aquarium. Joanie told the boys that Jeremy was her brother's friend. She wanted to be certain their relationship was going somewhere before she really introduced them. Joanie's brother even played along by spending the day with everyone at the aquarium.

Jeremy's and Joanie's boys hit it off. It wasn't long before Jeremy started calling Shaye, Joanie's youngest child, "mini-me." At one point during their trip to the aquarium, he let Jeremy carry him on his shoulders. Jeremy had grown up the oldest of boys, helping his brothers, Adam and Tanner, and this was second nature to him. Joanie was shocked by the way Shaye had taken to Jeremy so quickly; he usually wasn't comfortable around men and would only go to Joanie's dad and brother willingly.

Joanie brought her children to Jeremy's place in California one summer for what was supposed to be just a couple of weeks but turned out to be for most of the kids' summer vacation from school. Things went so well that Joanie and her boys visited again for Christmas vacation. Jeremy recalls, "The boys have been one of the biggest blessings in my life, even though in the beginning they were the part of our relationship that scared me the most. I wasn't sure I could take care of three boys. Just the thought was more than I wanted to think about."

But he decided to try to overcome his fear and make it work. Shaye, Sean, and Vance were still little guys when Jeremy and Joanie officially decided to live together in California as one big happy family. They found a little apartment, and once the boys finished their school year, Jeremy flew back to Texas to drive the U-Haul truck while Joanie drove her car.

On the way, the boys took turns riding with Jeremy and their mom. It was a fun time for everyone until only twelve hours into the drive when one of the truck's inner wheels blew. The vehicle ended up riding on a rim with fire sparks shooting out from underneath it. They had to wait alongside the road for hours, worried they'd have to send for another truck and repack it all, but in the end they got back on the road smoothly, no repacking or arguing required.

Jeremy knew that Joanie was meant for him, and he'd loved her boys from day one. Perhaps this overshadowed the reality of the situation. Jeremy never knew how hard it would be to transition from bachelor to family man. He now admits it was tougher than he'd ever imagined.

He'd never had a problem with loving his new family and feeling loved in return by them. In so many ways, they made it easy for him. But Jeremy, the child actor, was now responsible for everyone in this world that he and Joanie had created. He recalls how they all worked hard to make things work from the start. They took the boys on trips to the beach, going camping and fishing, and he taught them how to play sports. It was the life his fictional Seaver family lived on *Growing Pains*, to some extent.

However, Jeremy's drinking could not be suppressed for long. He found himself angry all the time, mostly without reason. He would alternately dote on the boys and then get angry and yell, confusing them. Joanie thought it best to put some distance between Jeremy and the kids, so she came up with all-day errands to keep the boys—and her—out of the house. He began to feel powerless and was full of self-loathing. He should be able to moderate his drinking, he felt; he was a strong person, and he should have the willpower to control himself. But no matter how hard he tried, he couldn't seem to overcome the addiction that was taking root deeper and deeper within him.

I had begun visiting with Kirk and Jeremy while they were filming in New Orleans, and when they returned home to Los Angeles, I continued to do so. I made an unannounced visit to Jeremy and Joanie's home during one of my visits to Los Angeles when I was staying with the Camerons. Joanie kept apologizing for Jeremy, and Jeremy kept telling me how much he loved me. He was pretty emotional, and it was clear he had been drinking. I finally began to realize what had been going on with Jeremy all this time.

With Joanie and the boys out of the room, Jeremy opened up

to me and shared some of his childhood experiences with me. I listened quietly, just trying to be there for him—to be a listening ear and a friend. It was hard to process this kind of darkness happening in my friend's life while it seemed like he was on top of the world. Everyone saw him grow up as the smiling Ben Seaver, but inside his real world, he had experienced things that would haunt him for decades. I remembered the words Mama had said before we flew to Los Angeles for my "wish." She had said, "Remember, even the actors who play those parts may not have the 'perfect' life in reality." She was so right.

I left Jeremy's home heartbroken. I cried most of the way back to the Camerons' house. Upon arrival, Kirk and Chelsea could see I was emotionally shaken by what I'd heard.

***

Jeremy was screaming internally throughout our whole conversation. He felt like a wreck. Looking back, he knows how lucky he was to have survived that time without losing those he loved.

Things got worse before they got better. Over time, Jeremy became a blackout drunk, and it was only getting worse. He believes he was passively trying to kill himself. "My desire to quit drinking came when I woke up after a night of blacking out to find Joanie sitting at the end of our bed looking pissed," he recalls. "My first question to her was, 'What did I do now?' It was a terrifying moment that I never wanted to face again. I never wanted to see that face again."

He knew something had to change. It was the start of Jeremy's quest to get sober.

Kirk had once told me that my first meeting with Jeremy, during my Starlight wish, was for me. He said my reconnecting with Jeremy, so many years later, would be for Jeremy. I didn't understand what Kirk was really saying when he made the comment; I didn't think I had anything to offer Jeremy. But in time, Kirk's words proved to be true.

CHAPTER TWENTY-TWO

MY DOCTORS, MY FRIENDS

My application letter to Baylor's residency program had started with the sentence "For as long as I can remember, I have always dreamed of being a physician at Texas Children's Hospital." I'd gone on to talk about my experience as a patient with the hospital. I hoped that would bring attention to my application. When I later interviewed with Dr. Ralph Feigin, physician in chief at Texas Children's Hospital and chair of the Department of Pediatrics at Baylor College of Medicine, he seemed genuinely happy to get to know me. He told me that he had been waiting for my interview since he read my application. My personal cover letter had caught his attention.

During my interview he'd told me that he wanted to see my dream of becoming a pediatric cardiologist come to fruition. While my scores were certainly contained within my application he and I never discussed them. When I had interviewed I was concerned that my performance on standardized exams might jeopardize my dream of working at Texas Children's Hospital from coming true.

Dr. Feigin and I talked about Texas Children's Hospital's logo change that had occurred about a decade earlier. One of my favorite shirts as a young child had been a T-shirt from Texas Children's Hospital with two children holding hands. This logo was eventually changed to a dot with three curvilinear lines surrounding it. As a pediatric cardiology patient, I thought the design was somehow related to echocardiography because it resembled the screen I would see on the monitor when this test was performed. I knew my idea could not be correct, so I asked Dr. Feigin about the symbol. He told me it was designed to convey the idea that patient care, education, and research are all centered around the patient—with the patient being represented by the dot in the middle.

Not once did we discuss my test scores. I worried that they would impact my qualifying for residency there. It was almost like he had forgotten to do so.

But Dr. Feigin had an excellent memory. As I began my residency there I realized I would be working with him often. We would present cases to him, and he would walk us through a differential diagnosis for the patient from memory. He impressively recited potential diagnoses in alphabetical order. He could even quote exact page numbers from his textbook or from journal articles he had read. Needless to say his intelligence intimidated me.

Dr. Feigin offered an opportunity for a resident to spend a month with him, one on one, to see what it was like to chair one of the most successful pediatric departments in the country. The monthlong experience was known as "The Feigin Elective." Many of my classmates had requested the privilege of observing Dr. Feigin in action. I had never asked for a month of one-on-one time with him but I got one anyway. Although I was nervous about the assignment, spending a month with Dr. Feigin was truly fascinating.

One morning he called my apartment before I had even started my day to suggest I come to the hospital a little early, because he was meeting with the director of the U.S. Centers for Disease Control and Prevention. At other times during my month with him, I would be asked to leave his office so that he could speak to President George W. Bush privately on the phone. Because of his expertise in infectious disease he helped establish the U.S. biodefense policy. He shared many stories and anecdotes from his career with me during the time we spent together. He told me that he had once been brought to the White House to be offered the position of Surgeon General. He'd declined the offer but he shared an amusing story about how he had been given a towel with the White House emblem on it as a gift. He worried about flying home with it for fear someone would think he had stolen it.

I did not understand why Dr. Feigin had selected me for his one-on-one mentorship until he invited me to go to a donor luncheon with him. The hospital was in the midst of a capital fund-raising campaign. During my Feigin Elective month I was asked to attend several investor meetings with Dr. Feigin. In the first meeting one of the potential investors asked about medicine expanding into fetal surgery. The man phrased the question doubtfully, as if it were an area of medicine that would best remain in the category of science fiction.

Dr. Feigin turned to me and asked if he could share my story. I nodded enthusiastically. *Would I mind? Of course not!*

He told the investors about how as a young child I had undergone open-heart surgery by Dr. Denton Cooley at Texas Children's Hospital. He shared the history of how open-heart surgery in children had begun and explained that the first several patients had died during surgery. He added that if medicine had not pressed forward I would likely not be there with them to share my story. When the conversation ended I realized very quickly that my time with him that month, and perhaps at Baylor itself, was not a coincidence. My presence there was helping him—and it was helping me, too. Medicine was progressing and the assumed prognosis of my disease was changing. By learning more about the progression of medicine, I was working to support the future generations of patients who would deal with heart disease.

I occasionally helped interview residency applicants with Dr. Feigin. During these interviews he usually mentioned test scores, which made me wonder why my interview had been different. I finally came right out and asked him.

Dr. Feigin responded, "I knew you had qualities that couldn't be measured on standardized exams because of your experiences as a patient." He said he knew I would succeed in the program and be a good doctor, despite my exam score, because of my history and my drive. My evaluation from my month with Dr. Feigin noted that I had helped update a chapter in his infectious disease textbook while helping raise over a million dollars for the hospital's expansion. His generosity and mentorship were invaluable.

Less than perfect test scores didn't keep Dr. Vargo from thinking highly of me as a candidate for acceptance to Baylor, either. He knew my dean's letter from Tulane had put me in the top half of my class, a requirement to be accepted to Baylor's pediatric program. The dean of each medical school writes a summary letter for each graduate, describing how they performed academically, how they related to others, and anything that makes them unique among their peers. The letter presented my successes and a statement about my potential. Four hundred applied annually. About thirty residents were matched into Baylor's program the year I applied.

He was not surprised that I was one of them. Neither was he caught off guard by my drive to improve my knowledge so that I could become board certified in both pediatrics and pediatric cardiology. Since he had been with me from the time I was a little boy, lying on his cath lab table, asking to remain awake while he worked on my heart, Dr. Vargo knew how driven I was.

While I was at Baylor he helped steer me toward my goal. When I started my residency, he became my academic advisor—but decided to have another doctor become my pediatric cardiologist. Dr. Vargo realized he could not be both my advisor and my cardiologist, and that's why he chose Dr. Ben Eidem to be my physician. Dr. Eidem was best suited for the job because he had trained at Mayo Clinic in pediatric cardiology, and that is where I had my last open-heart surgery during medical school.

As I finished up my pediatric residency and it came time to apply for fellowships in pediatric cardiology, I only interviewed at four places: Baylor, Mayo Clinic, Cincinnati Children's Hospital, and Vanderbilt. Even though I had always dreamed of working at Texas Children's Hospital, I had a hard time deciding if I should rank Baylor or Mayo Clinic first in the match. I eventually made an appointment with Dr. Feigin to discuss my options. He wanted to see me stay at Baylor, but he could understand my desire to be trained at both institutions, since I had been a patient at both. Dr. Feigin eventually told me that he would "loan me" to Mayo Clinic if I would promise to consider coming back to Texas Children's Hospital once I had completed my training. Interestingly enough, by the time I began my fellowship at Mayo

Clinic, Dr. Eidem had transferred from Texas Children's Hospital to Mayo Clinic, where he served as my pediatric cardiology fellowship program director.

It was more than a coincidence that Dr. Vargo was my advisor during my residency and Dr. Eidem was my program director during my fellowship. Both had been my physicians. Both had the distinction of knowing me inside and out. I had become securely connected to them through different points at different times in life. But they weren't the only two doctors with whom I shared this kind of relationship. I had this same special connection with Dr. Fernando Stein at Texas Children's Hospital and Dr. Allison Cabalka at Mayo Clinic.

Dr. Stein has spent his entire career as a medical doctor in pediatric intensive care at Baylor College of Medicine and Texas Children's Hospital. At the time of this writing, he was president of the American Academy of Pediatrics, a national organization that represents seventy thousand pediatricians, and has received about ninety awards over the course of his career. However, he will tell you that his greatest rewards amount to two. The first is whenever a parent offers him their child and asks him to take care of them, and the second is whenever a student offers himself and asks to learn from him. Dr. Stein takes both very seriously. As it turns out I have been both his patient and his student.

One day when we were making rounds, Dr. Stein inquired how I was so sure that I wanted to be a pediatric cardiologist. After I told him my story he asked for the date of my surgery as a child. He told me that he may have taken care of me after my surgery. I thought the conversation would end there, but after rounds, Dr. Stein asked me to walk with him.

"Throughout my fellowship, I kept a written record of all of my patients," he said, pointing to a display case at the entrance of the progressive care unit that contained historical medical equipment and books. He opened the case and pulled out an old book. It contained a record, much like a diary, of the patients he had cared for as a trainee, including their diagnoses and any complications. We found my name among the entries from November 1979. It was confirmed. As an intensive care fellow at Texas Children's Hospital he had cared for me when I was admitted to the ICU following my first open-heart surgery when I was two years old. He was yet another person whom God placed in my life at one point, only to have them reappear at a later time in a different role.

He continued as my supervisor for two separate month-long rotations during my three years at Baylor. Today, we cross paths occasionally. Our relationship has been that of learner and teacher. The way he sees it, in medicine the student learns by becoming an apprentice to his mentor until he's ready to start the work on his own. Dr. Stein has referred to my relationship with Dr. Vargo to drive the point home. Knowing us both, he has observed our apparent fondness for each other and my ability to learn from the man I looked up to growing up.

Dr. Stein helped organize a photo opportunity with me being flanked by Dr. Vargo and Dr. Cooley, my pediatric cardiologist and my pediatric cardiothoracic surgeon, respectively. I brought a copy of Dr. Cooley's memoir with me, subtitled "World's Greatest Surgeon,"—it was the copy Mama had purchased two decades earlier in the hospital's gift shop when my first heart surgery was performed. He signed it: *To Brandon, with sincere respect and congratulations on your career. Denton A. Cooley, MD.*

"Have you had any more surgeries since the one I performed?" he then asked.

"I had a second surgery at Mayo in June 2001."

"Did it give you more energy?"

I told him it had.

"Placebo effect," he quipped. He, Dr. Vargo, and I had a good laugh as a photographer captured the moment—today it is one of my most prized mementos from my medical education. It is physical proof that dreams do come true.

As crazy as it was to discover that Dr. Stein had provided care to me in the past, it was not the first time I had met a physician I did not know who had previously played a role in my care. When I was discharged from Mayo Clinic following my heart surgery in 2001, I noticed that my discharge medications were prescribed by Dr. David Cable, but his name was not familiar to me. About two years later, when I did a family medicine rotation in a town near Jena, I was surprised to find a sign in the foyer of Rapides Regional Medical Center welcoming Dr. David Cable to the hospital's staff. I recognized him when I ran into him in doctor's dining; once I saw him, I remembered that he had made rounds with Dr. Puga each day after my surgery. Dr. Cable had been a thoracic surgery trainee at the time, and he had helped care for me during and after my surgery.

I returned to Mayo Clinic for a checkup during my senior year of medical school. That's when, with Dr. Allison Cabalka's help, I turned the need for a follow-up appointment into an opportunity to do an away rotation at Mayo Clinic so that my medical insurance would pay for my evaluation. That was in 2003. When it came time to apply for fellowship, I ranked the pediatric cardiology program at Mayo Clinic at the top of my list. I found out I had been matched at Mayo Clinic on June 14, 2006, which was the five-year anniversary of my surgery there. It seemed meant to be.

During my first week of fellowship, I arrived early to our

combined surgical conference because I wanted to make sure I could find the room where the meeting was held. Before the conference began, Dr. Puga chose a chair only a few seats away from me. He kept glancing at me throughout the meeting, and afterward he introduced himself and asked, "Have we met before?"

I laughed and jokingly replied, "Dr. Puga, you have seen parts of me that even *I* have never seen," before explaining that I had been his patient. He had physically touched my heart with his hands, and because of his skill as a surgeon, I'd been able to pursue my dreams. It was a special moment for both of us.

Each year of my fellowship Dr. Vargo made a trip to Minnesota to attend the annual conference in echocardiography held at Mayo Clinic. He always took the time to talk to the faculty about my progress. Some of them jokingly called him my faculty advisor emeritus because he still took such an interest in my progress even after I'd moved on from Texas Children's Hospital. There was an out-of-print book called *The Science and Practice of Pediatric Cardiology* that I wanted. Dr. Vargo was one of the textbook's authors. When I asked him if he knew where I could get a copy of the text, he offered to send me his copy. It is a prized possession for sure. It has his initials, TV, on the spine of the book and is inscribed,

"*Dear Brandon,*

It is my pleasure to present this text to you. You are a real inspiration to me—you have accomplished so much already, and I know more will come."

As a fellow, I ended up working closely with Dr. Allison Cabalka, the physician who performed my predischarge echocardiogram in 2001 after my open-heart surgery. From this short interaction, I liked her enough to ask if she would become my pediatric cardiologist at Mayo Clinic, and during my fellowship, she became one of my mentors.

Dr. Cabalka spends much of her "free time" traveling the globe to provide care for pediatric heart patients who otherwise would not have access to the care they need. Sometimes she travels with a team of physicians to perform surgeries and cath-based procedures on these patients in their home countries. While there, the team of doctors often identify patients with more complex defects who need to travel to the United States for surgery. I had the opportunity to care for patients brought through the Children's Heart Project of Samaritan's Purse, a Christian humanitarian organization that provides aid to people in physical need. The patients who came through this program could not have the surgery they required in their home country. One of the countries the Heart Project served was Mongolia, and many of the Mongolian patients shared my diagnosis—they came to Mayo Clinic for repair of Tetralogy of Fallot.

While medical centers in the United States typically repair patients with Tetralogy of Fallot during infancy, these patients hadn't had access to an early repair. Many of them were older by the time they traveled to Mayo Clinic, some even in their teens. Many of them had a bluish tint to their skin or had trouble walking long distances. It was an opportunity to see how profoundly I could have been affected by my heart defect if I hadn't been born in a place where early repair had become the norm.

Sometime later, Kirk Cameron interviewed one of the executives at Samaritan's Purse about the Children's Heart Project for the Trinity Broadcast Network. Although Kirk didn't mention me by name, he did talk about his friend at Mayo Clinic who helped care for these patients. Shortly thereafter, I received an invitation from Samaritan's Purse to travel to Mongolia for a week with a team scheduled to perform heart surgeries there. I was never quite sure if it was Kirk's interview or Dr. Cabalka's connections that resulted in this opportunity.

I traveled to Ulaanbaatar, Mongolia's capital, to volunteer for two weeks. During the first week I helped a pediatric cardiologist perform echos on patients to help identify those who needed intervention. By the second week the full team had arrived (nurses, surgeons, and all the other specialists required for the operations), and surgeries were performed. The Mongolian team would work alongside us to develop their skills and improve outcomes. Throughout the two weeks, I had the opportunity to see some of the patients I had cared for in the United States when they came in for a checkup. Our team stayed together at a hotel in the capital. We sampled the local food and walked around the city like tourists when we were off duty. I had never seen anything like it.

I would have declined such an offer to go to a third-world country were it not for Dr. Cabalka. I had often been reluctant to travel outside of the United States due to my nervousness about the risk of being away from medical care. However, I felt comfortable going to Mongolia for two weeks because Dr. Cabalka was also going to be there and I did not want to deny myself such an opportunity. Like many of the physicians in my life, she has played multiple roles in getting me to where I am today.

CHAPTER TWENTY-THREE

REUNITING FICTIONAL
TV BROTHERS

My first few times at Kirk's home had given me the opportunity to see how a family of eight functioned. With my sister Brenda being thirteen years my senior, I had pretty much grown up as an only child. For most of my childhood and adolescent life, it was just Mama and me.

When Kirk first introduced all six of his children to me, he had made up a fake name for each of them. As I was trying to remember all of the names, the kids started laughing, saying, "Dad, you are doing it wrong." Kirk then introduced me to his youngest children and had the older ones introduce themselves. Jack, his oldest who was around six at the time, took my hand and gave me a tour of the Cameron home. Getting to spend time with Kirk's family while they were filming in New Orleans had solidified my connection to them.

The first time I'd stayed with the Camerons, they had turned their playroom into a guest room. At 7:00 a.m. sharp the following day I could hear the kids' feet hit the floor all at once, and the next thing I knew they were knocking on my door to see if I was ready to play. I felt very much at home with Kirk, Chelsea, and their kids. We would do simple family things when I was there. We would go on hikes or make trips to the beach. Nothing was extravagant. Meal time was one of my favorite times. Kirk would say grace and give a short devotional before our meal. The kids would usually take turns asking me questions throughout dinner.

Kirk asked me to help with home improvement projects like painting his office or removing flower beds in their backyard so the kids would have more room to run and play. These ordinary things made my visits extraordinary and made me very happy. I came to feel as if I belonged. I have to pause here to say that truly one of my favorite things about staying with the Camerons is the fact that I am just able to fall into being a part of their family. It reminds me of when I would stay with my friend Matt and his family during my college years. I always appreciated that Kirk and Chelsea didn't change their routine because I was there. Years later, they built a guest cottage on their property, which I would get to stay in, too.

My involvement on the board of directors for Starlight Children's Foundation resulted in a few visits a year to the Los Angeles area, which gave me an opportunity to spend time with both Kirk and Jeremy. Whenever I had a Starlight event in Los Angeles, I would often email the dates to Kirk and Jeremy to see if they were going to be in town.

On one of my early trips Jeremy and his family came over to Kirk's house, and Jeremy cooked chicken carbonara for all of us. A few months later, while I was in a patient's room while on overnight call, I noticed the television set playing some show about the "100 Greatest TV Kids." While going over my notes I could hear Kirk on TV talking about how Jeremy had recently come to his house to cook dinner for his family.

I got very emotional and excused myself from the patient's room for just a moment. I knew Kirk and Jeremy didn't typically hang out together. So in some way I had played a role in bringing them closer. I began to see how my wish as a child was having an effect on all of us.

On my second trip to see Jeremy, his mom, Sonja, made a point to sit beside me on the couch and put her arm around me before Jeremy had even started his day. She thanked me for coming—and even for loving her son. She told me that Jeremy cared about me and that I was a part of their family. It was a special moment for me; I felt she had fully accepted me as Jeremy's true friend, and I was glad to be there for him.

I especially enjoyed when the Cameron family shared stories from Camp Firefly. A few times, Chelsea even asked me to help identify kids who would benefit from their camp. One time, she contacted me during my time at Mayo Clinic while I was on an outreach trip to North Dakota. I knew Chelsea has a very special place in her heart for kids with cancer, and between patients, I stopped by the cancer clinic down the hall and inquired if they could help identify kids for a friend's camp. I didn't mention Kirk or Chelsea or even the camp's name, but they told me they had a young boy and his family that they thought would be a good fit. I took down a contact name and number, and told them I would have someone from camp contact them.

Chelsea called me that evening to tell me that something very special had happened. The child who was recommended had already been suggested by another source. Chelsea said that she knew this family had to be selected because they had never received the same child's name from two separate sources. This young man and his family ended up becoming very close to the Cameron family.

I called Kirk one Thanksgiving while I was living in Minnesota. I was surprised when he told me that he and his family were in Houston to visit the young boy and his family at one of the hospitals in the medical center there. Even though I had never met the young child or his family, I felt a connection to them. I was certainly thankful that God had used me to help bring some new friends into their life. I knew what it must be like to spend a holiday in the hospital.

While I was completing my fellowship at Mayo Clinic, some friends from Minnesota, Pam and Chuck, were planning to be in Los Angeles at the same time I was. I had met them at church the first Sunday I lived in Minnesota. Chuck was a local firefighter, and they'd invited Mama and me to have lunch with them after services and visit their family's farm. We became friends, and they even hosted some of the children who came to Mayo Clinic from Mongolia through Samaritan's Purse for heart surgery. They were in town for a Firefighters for Christ conference. I was supposed to meet them for dinner on my last night in L.A., but Kirk suggested I invite them to have dinner with his family at their home instead. The kids didn't want me to be away that evening, since I was leaving the next day.

Pam and Chuck agreed to come to dinner, but I purposely didn't tell them in whose home I was staying. *Growing Pains* had been off the air for a while; perhaps they wouldn't even recognize Kirk's name. And if they did, I didn't want to make them nervous. But of course, they immediately recognized Kirk. Just the night before they had screened his movie *Fireproof* at the conference. Chuck and I had many good laughs back in Minnesota about "that one time I had invited him to a friend's house for dinner in California."

Over the years, and especially when all of the children were young, Kirk and Chelsea would call me with health-related questions. On more than one occasion, Kirk's children have introduced me to friends as *their* "24-7 doctor." Kirk and Chelsea may not realize it, but that feeling of belonging is one of the greatest gifts they have given me.

I must admit there are times, even with friends, when I'm afraid to call or email because I worry they will not call or email me back. It's definitely a holdover from those years of missed communication with Daddy—the hang-ups, disguised voices, and calls that never came. However, with Kirk and Jeremy both, God has given me a sense of peace. I know they will continue to call back. I know they will be a part of my life for many years to come. I have also formed close bonds with many of the Starlight Children's Foundation staff and board members. These relationships confirm the fact that God understood the true intention behind my wish, all those years ago. I am a member of a very large extended family that has taught me that relationships don't end—they just evolve and hopefully become stronger with time.

***

During my residency at Baylor, I was invited to strengthen the role that I had with Starlight Children's Foundation.

Although Starlight's wish-granting program ended in 2005, the organization's other programs fulfill wishes in other ways. Every year in the United States alone, between ten and twenty million children suffer from a chronic illness or serious medical condition. That's a lot of kids. So Starlight scales up its support with larger programs that are designed to bring laughter, fun, and joy to as many kids as possible. Starlight Brave Gowns, Starlight Fun Centers, Starlight Sites, and its philanthropy platform provide the best in entertainment, education, and technology to children at more than seven hundred children's hospitals and other pediatric facilities all across the country.

Under the leadership of then chief executive officer Paula Van Ness, who worked for Starlight for six years, I became a Global Ambassador and a member of the board of directors. My job was to represent the organization and spread goodwill on behalf of it by sharing my own personal story.

Every year Starlight has held a gala or some special event to raise money. Starlight's cofounder Peter Samuelson had a big vision that matched his big heart. In addition to Starlight, Peter has founded other charitable organizations. He saw early on that there was a great opportunity to use technology in medicine and created Starbright, which provided an online community where kids in hospitals could chat initially via video and later via online chat rooms with other kids across the nation. He also designed webisodes to educate children about their illnesses while entertaining them. In 2004, Starlight merged with Starbright. Steven Spielberg had been associated with Starbright, and he remains the chairman emeritus of the Starlight Global Board of Directors.

During my time as a pediatric resident I returned to the Beverly Hilton Hotel to help honor Spielberg for his work at the organization. I was invited to tell my story to the gala attendees before introducing him. I introduced myself as a doctor and began to tell my story, framing it around an anonymous little boy and his caring mother. I shared how the boy had grown up to work with the doctors who had cared for him. I didn't reveal that the little boy was me until the end, just before introducing Spielberg.

I'm told there wasn't a dry eye in the ballroom. Without a doubt it was a meaningful presentation that showed just what a big impact the organization could make.

When Starlight and Starbright merged I became one of thirty-five board members. I was the youngest and the only one who had been served by the organization. I never took this for granted. I continue to show how much I genuinely appreciate the foundation for what it did for me. And there have been many ways I found to accomplish this.

When I was in medical school we were required to do community service. I volunteered as a Make-A-Wish wish granter. In my last two years of medical school I also served on the board of directors of the Louisiana chapter of the Make-A-Wish Foundation. I was asked to review their local wish-granting guidelines. This would have been in the early 2000s. I was surprised to find that Tetralogy of Fallot was specifically listed as a diagnosis that automatically qualified for a wish. I didn't have the heart to remove it or even suggest a change in its status even though I was living proof that the condition was no longer terminal thanks to advances in medicine. I was asked to attend the Super Bowl in New Orleans that followed the 9/11 attacks with all of the Make-A-Wish kids who had asked to attend the game as their wish. Being with them felt like I was giving back.

Starlight honored the Hilton family for their commitment to Starlight at its annual gala. I thought Kathy Hilton, the noted philanthropist and mother of Nicky and Paris, was a very classy lady. But what impressed me most was watching how the Starlight kids interacted with her. I have yet to see another public personality know Starlight kids by name in the way Kathy did. During the evening's program a young girl with cancer described going to the Hilton home where Kathy and her daughters would hold tea parties for some of the Starlight girls. She said that one of her favorite memories was playing duck-duck-goose with Miss Nicky and Miss Paris. It was very touching and it made me realize that the media doesn't often write the whole story on the celebrities it covers—or even get it right.

Over the years Jeremy has attended a few Starlight events with me including a Starlight fund-raiser at Kathy Hilton's home. They auctioned him off as a celebrity chef for an in-home cooking experience. He went with me to Starlight's annual gala one year where we met a family who had given money to Starlight from their parents' estate in honor of their sister. Their sister had died in childhood, and her wish had been to meet Mr. T from the TV show *The A-Team*. Mr. T had stayed in touch with them and, amazingly, was there with them at the charity event. Jeremy and I both took time to speak to the family. It was so poignant to see how Mr. T had impacted not only this wish kid's life but the lives of her siblings, as well. For them and for me, Starlight had been like a water ripple started by the pebble of a wish that just kept on expanding. In time the ripple even touched those in my birth family. Brenda's youngest son Logan was born with a birth defect the day before I learned I was selected to receive a wish. Ultimately Logan got his own wish from Starlight.

***

Growing up I would never have imagined that because of this organization, my life would intertwine with Jeremy's. I never could have imagined that he and his family would truly become an extended family for me. I would never have imagined that my work would bring me to Corpus Christi, Texas, where Joanie, Jeremy's fiancée, was raised. I have since become close with Joanie, her sons, and even her parents. As I went to dinner at their home one night, I was shocked to realize it was the twenty-sixth anniversary of my wish. Who could have foreseen it?

I can't ever forget the wise words Kirk shared with me in New Orleans—that my reconnecting with Jeremy wasn't about *me*. It was about something greater. Eight years after reconnecting with Jeremy I received an email that would expand and strengthen our relationship. I can honestly say that at different stages, both of our lives have been blessed by the other.

CHAPTER TWENTY-FOUR

A LIFE-AND-DEATH DECISION

I f I were asked to describe my life's purpose it would be this: to help others to the degree I have been helped. The gratitude I feel toward the doctors who have seen to my health, the family members who have been there all along, and the mother who pushed me to succeed at anything upon which I set my heart's desire make that purpose a practical necessity. I make an effort to help others whenever it is within my power to do so.

This is not always easy. After my friend Matt met and married Tiffany during our senior year, they wanted to start having children. While I was in medical school they called to tell me that their second child, a baby named Annabelle Bliss, had been born with complications. Over the next few days Annabelle was diagnosed with hypoxic ischemic encephalopathy, a condition that occurs when the brain is deprived of an adequate oxygen supply. Their little girl died soon afterward.

When I first got word of the baby's condition I knew I needed to help in any way I could. I had worked with a number of families who had received tough diagnoses concerning their children. It's never easy to see parents make heartbreaking decisions. Matt and Tiffany had a tremendous decision to make. As painful as it was I discussed over the phone with Matt the option of withdrawing support. I passed on something one of my attending physicians, while working in the pediatric intensive care unit as a resident, once told me: "Sometimes, the most loving thing someone can do for their child is to do nothing."

Those words seemed uncaring when I first heard them, but they have stuck with me through the years. As a physician, you want to do something to help but doing too much may only prolong suffering and not improve quality of life. It was without a doubt one of the most difficult conversations I have ever had, but I knew I needed to step up and be there for my friend. I could do so not only because I treated children on a daily basis but also because I had lived a significant part of my early life thinking about dying young. I had faced my own mortality and, in the end, trusted that God is all-knowing and all-caring. God cared for Matt and Tiffany and their baby girl. I have no doubt of that. I also have no doubt that He allowed Matt to be used in my life so I could be used in his.

While I was in fellowship at Mayo Clinic in Rochester, Minnesota, I heard from Coach Burgess, my sophomore-year high school biology teacher. In 2007, the same year Matt and Tiffany's infant daughter died, his daughter Anna came down with an illness that local doctors couldn't diagnose. The family made the decision to bring Anna to Mayo Clinic for evaluation. Nancie Corley, who had taught me high school chemistry, told Coach Burgess I was currently working at Mayo Clinic and could possibly help.

He called to explain that Anna was having unexplainable episodes of dizziness and light-headedness. Once I had reviewed her medical records, I called Coach and let him know that I would help in any way I could. I even had an extra car they could use while they were in town. I did my best to take care of them as they focused on the problems Anna was facing.

Before long, a medical team at Mayo Clinic pinpointed what was going on. Anna had POTS—postural orthostatic tachycardia syndrome—a condition in which the brain and automatic nervous system fight each other. Anna's doctor compared it to a glitch in a computer program. The syndrome can bring one's heart rate up and blood pressure down. When the condition started in Anna she had begun blacking out. There's no known cause for POTS, and no full cure. For some patients, with time, the condition simply disappears as suddenly as it appeared. For others, it can seriously impact their lives.

Anna was homebound and homeschooled. Since her diagnosis at Mayo, she had been in and out of the hospital. I remained in touch throughout her illness. The one thing I could do to help was to relate with what she was going through. There's a mental aspect to her diagnosis, just as there was with mine. She was missing out on activities her classmates got to enjoy as normal teenagers; she worried that they would not remember her. I tried to be an encouragement whenever I talked to her. Like me at her age, Anna threw herself into her studies. She had plans to give back and, in her own way, try to help others. Anna wanted to become a life coach or an onsite trauma psychologist because of what she had been through. Anna died on her nineteenth birthday from complications following a medical procedure. But I hope that in my own way, I was able to make her disease more bearable and to give her hope.

In late May 2015, Dr. Ramu's wife had to have open-heart surgery at Texas Children's Hospital for a congenital heart problem.

Dr. Ramu had taught me physical chemistry at Louisiana Tech University, and before his wife's surgery, Dr. Ramu sent her cardiac MRI to me, asking my thoughts. I told them it was something that had to be corrected.

By the time Dr. Ramu and his wife arrived at Texas Children's Hospital for the surgery, I had already asked the physician in chief to look after them; he in turn asked the institution's chief of cardiology to check on them during their stay, which made them feel they were well cared for. That kind of help made all the difference for the professor who loved his wife deeply and desperately wanted her to receive great care.

It is an amazing thing to be able to touch people's lives, making them feel heard—safe and secure, even when facing the unknown. Over time I am glad I could do the things I did for Matt, Anna, and Dr. and Mrs. Ramu. Being a sounding board, reviewing files, and making introductions were all little things that had a big impact. I understand that.

When Alan Thicke passed away in December 2016, I mourned the death of one of America's great TV dads. I knew that if *I* was struggling with the loss, then Jeremy was suffering more. I reached out to Jeremy and tried to be there for him. I was glad that the *Growing Pains* cast was close enough to come together as a family and support each other through a difficult time. A few days after Alan's funeral, Jeremy and Joanie came to Louisiana to spend a few days with me.

In my own way, I'm paying it forward, which is what I believe we're all here to do anyway. I was honored that I could do this for others and their families. I was humbled when God allowed me to do it for mine.

My sister, Brenda, long suffered from a medical condition called hyperparathyroidism, which is associated with psychosis.

On top of that, she was in a volatile relationship. As time went on, she would show up to work at the Cracker Barrel showing the symptoms of her relationship, doing her best to disguise them from coworkers and customers with makeup and a smile. Finally her boss, Jarrett, decided to intervene. He knew Brenda had a brother living out of state, so he bought her a bus ticket so she could get away and stay with me. Jarrett's pay it forward was to make sure my sister got on that bus, which is why he not only purchased her way out of town but also drove her to the station.

Brenda left her home like a thief in the night with just a change of clothes and Kirk Cameron's autobiography in her bag. I had told Kirk Brenda's story while it was happening, and he often prayed for her, asking God to rescue her from the bad relationship she was in. Brenda knew about Kirk's prayers, which is why his book became her comfort during the long bus ride.

Brenda called me from the bus station to tell me she was on her way. I had a little more than twenty-four hours to prepare for her arrival. I picked up Brenda at the bus station in Minneapolis on Father's Day in 2008. (Because of that, to this day, Brenda calls me on Father's Day just to wish me a "happy day.") Upon her arrival, she explained that she wasn't feeling well after the long ride, and I diagnosed a blood clot in her leg. We went straight from the bus station to the hospital, where she ended up staying for a week and a half. It ended up being a blessing, as the hospital social worker helped identify programs that could help her.

I spent a lot of time with Brenda when she was in Minnesota. She lived in Rochester during the last two years of my fellowship and she even stayed there for a year after I left. Growing up I had always considered Brenda to be my closest friend despite the age difference between us. I knew she had sacrificed a lot for me over the years. When I stayed home alone while Mama worked she fed me and drove me to all my school events. I had even heard stories of how she had to take me as a small child on her high school dates just to keep me from becoming upset and turning blue. I knew Brenda had not had the opportunities that I did growing up—too much time and energy had to be devoted to me in her late adolescence. Yet she had always adored me and treated me well. I was more than happy to try to help because I just wanted to have my sister back. Plus I knew that if I didn't, her situation was severe enough that she might not survive it.

During my remaining years of fellowship Brenda and I spent a lot of time together. Having my sister in town was definitely a distraction during the last two years of medical training but many of the doctors who trained me at Mayo Clinic had also taken care of me as a patient, so they were invested in seeing me succeed. They helped where they could.

Brenda began working as a waitress at a local restaurant. I would often go there for dinner, sit in her section, and then take her home after work. We even found ourselves undertaking a journaling project about what had happened in her relationship.

"It would be helpful if you could write down everything you remember," said the voice on the other line at the sheriff's office. "It could help your case. It could also assist another victim sometime down the line."

Journaling, most importantly, was a source of healing for Brenda. And so she wrote about her wounds with the help of her younger brother. She would tell me what she had gone through and I would type it out. These journaling sessions often left us both in tears. I was glad to be able to help her, even though hearing the details was incredibly painful.

In some ways, having Brenda with me in Minnesota was like having a teenager. I wanted to take care of her and make sure she was safe. But it was work to make sure she didn't get into any trouble. I worried about her like a parent. She was recovering from a difficult and repressive relationship, and there were times when she didn't make good choices. There were situations where I had to use tough love like the time I made her walk a few miles home to emphasize the fact that I had boundaries. Brenda had taken a cab to catch the free bus going to the local casino because I had plans with a friend that evening and was unavailable to have dinner with her. But when she returned later that evening with no money for a cab she called and woke me up. She asked me to pick her up where the bus had dropped her off. When I told her that I wouldn't come she called Mama, and Mama tried to convince me to get her. I had already made up my mind that I wouldn't go. I knew I had to take a stand or I would set a precedent that she could make irresponsible choices or not take accountability for her actions. Sometimes life's choices have consequences.

It was important to me to make it clear I wasn't obligated to help her and that she would have to do her part: maintain a job, see a psychiatrist, and keep a restraining order in place on her ex-boyfriend if I was going to help. Drawing boundaries and having some distance were very important steps in my own ability to function at my task of finishing school, as well as be a whole enough person to help her.

I knew Brenda was expecting a settlement from her divorce, and we had found the perfect used car for her: a 2002 Volkswagen Beetle Turbo. We returned from a great test drive, ready to buy, only to find that another sales manager, whose nametag read "Burl," had sold it to someone else *while we were driving it.* I had never heard of such a thing; I began to suspect we were being played so he could earn extra commission. My sister had gone through so much, and I couldn't stand the thought of someone else taking advantage of her. The conversation grew heated. I complained to another manager on the sales floor. To this day Brenda still laughs about me shouting, "Bite me, Burl. This isn't over!" and stalking out of the dealership.

But the next day, the other sales manager called back—the problem had been resolved and we could buy the car at a discounted price! After that near miss, I didn't want to lose another opportunity to buy it, so I purchased the car in my name with the agreement that Brenda would pay the car off once she received her settlement.

One day, after a disagreement she decided that she wasn't going to pay for the car. I told her she wasn't holding up her end of the deal. When I returned to pick her up from work, she noticed I had slapped a "for sale" sign on the vehicle. She didn't want me to sell the car. Eventually, she received her settlement, and we were able to transfer the car to her name. It was a difficult situation but in the end she knew I was just looking out for her.

But there were also the times when living near Brenda was simply *fun*. While she was there, I saw my sister almost every day. She and I would eat together, or if she was working, I would go to the restaurant. We took trips to "the cities," as well. Minneapolis–St. Paul was a great place to spend time when I wasn't on call and Brenda was free. We'd visit my friends and colleagues from Mayo Clinic—a favorite memory was our annual visit to Dr. Cabalka's home to help decorate her sixteen-foot Christmas tree.

I helped Brenda for two years—the time she needed to start to heal from what she had suffered. My amazing sister made it through and learned to pay it forward. Through all the journaling she did Brenda found her voice and a message to give to others. She knows now that you don't have to live in abusive situations. There are avenues of help—people you can go to, like Jarrett and me. There are programs available to those who are living in abusive relationships. Her strongest admonition is not to be afraid to tell someone. She recalls talking to a girl who came into the restaurant black and blue, trying to hide her own scars. Brenda gave her information on the Domestic Violence Help Line.

There were moments I couldn't be prouder of my big sister. Once, while making hospital rounds with Dr. Cabalka at St. Mary's Hospital, I discovered Brenda sitting with one of the Mongolian children, giving his family a much-needed break. I hadn't even known she was at the hospital. Brenda's youngest son Logan had several surgeries as a child, and Brenda helped care for me after both of my heart surgeries. I felt confident that she would take good care of the child while his mom took a break. Then, there was the time Coach Burgess, his wife Sherry, and Anna came to Mayo Clinic for Anna's diagnosis. Brenda really stepped up to take care of them and to help while they were in town. She even let them stay with her.

Brenda had a protective order placed on her ex-boyfriend even though she never again saw him until the day she went to court to renew it. Everyone said he wouldn't show up. But it was the third such hearing, and Brenda knew that the third time is usually a charm. She felt he would be there to fight the order, and he was.

It just so happened that she was preparing to go on a cruise to Alaska for two weeks the following Sunday. She flew to Seattle and met up with Mama and me before boarding the ship. It was August 2010, and I had finished my medical training a few months before and had moved to Texas. After her time in court knowing that her ex-boyfriend was somewhere in town, Brenda arranged to stay with my doctor and colleague Dr. Allison Cabalka from Mayo Clinic until it was time for her to fly out. Brenda stayed with Dr. Cabalka and her husband, Jeff, for three days without incident.

Today Brenda works at the Cracker Barrel in Alexandria. It's about an hour from home. There has never been another issue since that time. It's been more than five years since Brenda has seen or heard from the guy, and that says a lot about God's mercy and the power of answered prayer.

Brenda has a big heart, a great sense of humor, and like me, she's able to help others because of the help she's received. I find it interesting that Brenda and I have both played the role of "caregiver" for the other at different stages of life. It is probably one of the reasons why we remain so close. She and I both would not be where we are in life if it weren't for the love and compassion shown to us by others, and we both consider it a privilege when God uses us to help others.

CHAPTER TWENTY-FIVE

THANK GOD MAMA KEPT
MY REPORT CARDS

I walked out of my pediatric cardiology board exam full of frustration. I was so upset with myself. *How could I have failed this after so much work? How could I not finish in time?*

I had finished my fellowship at Mayo Clinic and set off to San Francisco in November of 2010 to take the boards. I was ready to really get going—to officially start my medical career. But I knew I had failed the exam as soon as I left the room because I didn't have enough time to complete it. I had to make quick guesses at many questions on the exam. I had not requested any accommodation for my learning disability because of my pride; I didn't want others in the room to see me as less bright because I needed extra time.

Later that day, my friend Poomi and I went to eat and explore the Fisherman's Wharf area of San Francisco where we stumbled across a group of street performers. I was surprised to recognize a face I had seen years ago: Orion Griffiths, whom Ashley Johnson had befriended in New Orleans all those years ago. I had met him on the very day I'd found out where I was going for my residency. I whispered the story to Poomi; I wondered if it was him. A few minutes later my question was answered. The performer approached a lady who was talking on her cell phone, took the phone, and told the person on the other end of the call, "This is Orion. You are interrupting my show. Please call your friend back later." I spoke to him after the performance and he was indeed the person I had met back in New Orleans.

God was once again showing His presence to me. He was letting me know that He was with me even in failure. He was reminding me not to get discouraged about my health issues or learning disability because He had made me perfectly for His purpose. I would eventually learn that several of my colleagues had also failed the exam on their first attempt. The exam was scored in a way that guaranteed that 20%–25% of first-time test takers would fail.

Unfortunately, the exam is only offered every other year, so I would have to wait until 2012 to retake it. I made a request for an accommodation that would give me additional time on the exam almost a year in advance of taking it. After waiting several months for a response to my request, I called for an update. I was told that my testing from medical school was considered to be out of date. I repeated the testing in February 2011. This time, even though my scores qualified me for Mensa membership, the examiner not only found me to have a reading disability but also diagnosed me with a nonverbal learning disorder, a condition that has some traits in common with Asperger syndrome, because of my pattern of scores on the IQ test he had administered.

I was shocked. When I compared my test results to those obtained when I was placed in the gifted and talented program in the eighth grade, the score pattern was similar but less pronounced than it was in my original testing. In fact, the examiner noted then that there was a "statistically significant difference" between key scores. This meant that my verbal scale IQ (which measures verbal reasoning and the ability to use past knowledge and experience) was much higher than my performance scale IQ (which measured overall visuospatial intellectual abilities).

However the American Board of Pediatrics (ABP) also refused the second round of tests, stating that the examiner's conclusions were invalid. "Nonverbal learning disability" is not a diagnosis in the *Diagnostic and Statistical Manual of Mental Disorders*, the common standard for diagnosing learning disorders. I obtained an additional battery of tests by a third examiner. Luckily Mama had kept my report cards and standardized test scores over the years. The third examiner was able to review all of the data and convince the ABP that my learning disability was developmental in nature. Just a few weeks before the exam the ABP finally agreed to provide me with the needed accommodation. Looking back, I realize it was only God who could trade beauty for ashes.

I passed my pediatric cardiology boards on my second attempt with no problems. In fact, my score was just within the top quartile. It was the first time I had scored above average on a major standardized medical exam. I could not wait to share the news with Dr. Vargo. Sadly, Dr. Feigin had passed away during my time at Mayo Clinic. I really wished I could have shared the news with him. Both men had believed in my potential as a physician despite my low standardized test scores, and that had always meant a lot to me.

I finally realized how pride had likely caused me years of needless worry. If I had just accepted the accommodations that were suggested perhaps I could have lived with less pressure and gained more confidence along the way. Sometimes going down the right path requires us to put aside our pride and simply ask for the help we need.

CHAPTER TWENTY-SIX

LIKE A FAIRY TALE...
UNTIL IT WASN'T

By this point in time, Jeremy Miller wasn't the only one who knew he was an alcoholic. It was clear to his family that he had a dangerous problem. Joanie, Sonja, and friends began to talk of an intervention. *How should they do it?* Joanie wondered. *Who should be involved?*

Jeremy wasn't oblivious to their worry. He tried to stop drinking, furious with himself for constantly disappointing those who loved him. He tried AA, a thirty-day rehab program, outpatient therapy, herbal and holistic therapy, and prayer, but his longest period of sobriety lasted just six weeks. Letting go of a strong addiction wasn't easy and when Jeremy was sober the feelings he'd worked so long to numb came flooding back. Jeremy needed the best kind of practical help in the worst kind of way. Fortunately for him, he had Joanie by his side.

Joanie was an incredibly supportive force for Jeremy. She'd also had her own share of troubles. She struggled growing up the daughter of a fundamental Baptist preacher, and she left her parents' home when she was eighteen. By the time she met Jeremy she was the mother of three young boys and in a marriage that could be emotionally volatile. She had become accustomed to being with a man who did not value her thoughts and feelings the way she wished. That was such a stark contrast to the TV sitcom actor she was getting to know in New Orleans. In fact, Jeremy seemed like no other man she had ever met before. In the very short period of time since they'd met she could see that not only did he care for her, but he was genuinely kind to her brother and cousins, too.

On their second date she told him everything. Jeremy listened intently to Joanie's story about her life and the situation she found herself in with her husband. Even before she had finished the story, however, Jeremy began to cry. Joanie was in awe. She wondered how he could care so much about a virtual stranger. But even if they had known each other for years, his reaction still would have taken her aback. She realized that up to this point she'd felt like no one had really ever cared for her.

Joanie tells the story of being a young girl on a church-sponsored singing bus tour with other girls her age. One day between venues the bus driver stopped at a park so everyone could get out and have lunch. While they were eating, a biracial couple sat at an adjacent picnic table. They were holding hands, looking very much in love. One of the girls on the tour saw them and started saying that the sight of the couple was disgusting. Joanie was half Filipino and the product of a mixed marriage herself so she naturally defended the unknown couple. She was met with anger. The preacher's wife, who was acting as chaperone, said that it was not only disgusting but out of God's order for the races to mix. Then she pointedly told Joanie that *she* was a mistake, too.

Joanie started to cry. The preacher's wife quickly reprimanded her. When her parents arrived for the group's evening performance, Joanie tried to tell them about the conversation. She begged them to remove her from the tour. But instead they left her on it. She recalls: "I started drifting away from the church and believing that the only one who would ever take care of me was me. It took years to change my thoughts on that and a bit longer to step back into a church. I did, when I understood that no matter what, I could trust God. And He helped me see that I could trust Jeremy by making me aware of Jeremy's genuine feelings for me."

After New Orleans and Joanie's full disclosure to Jeremy, she returned home only to have him ask her to come back the following weekend so that they could spend more time together. Her husband agreed, perhaps seeing it as an opportunity for Joanie to meet the rest of the *Growing Pains* cast. What he didn't know is that another trip to New Orleans would lead to the end of their marriage. Joanie had felt unloved by her husband for some time. She had even tried to leave her husband before but stuck it out for her kids. When Joanie returned to Texas, just two and a half weeks after she'd met Jeremy, she finally left her husband for good.

It's important to know the genesis of Jeremy and Joanie's relationship. Even though circumstances weren't optimal their relationship had a sense of destiny to it. Joanie was always of the mind-set that one should marry for life. But New Orleans—a place she didn't want to be in the first place—was the breaking point for a marriage that wasn't livable or healthy.

Jeremy told Joanie that he loved her first. She was happy to hear it but couldn't say it back because she was confused about her feelings and didn't want to say it unless she truly meant it.

When Joanie and her boys moved out to California to live

with Jeremy, they were all ready to start anew. The kids came up with the idea to change their last name—they wanted to be called "Miller." So Joanie made it legal. When they went to the court-house to get a new last name, Joanie allowed her sons to pick new middle names, too. The youngest chose "Jeremy" for his middle name. It wasn't that they were trying to do away with the fact that they had a father in Texas. They were just ready to move on past the hurt.

Joanie had been through so much that she was a bit reluctant to trust Jeremy at first. Though she had moved herself and her kids to California, she was always waiting for the other shoe to drop. She would pick fights to see how he would react, she says, "but Jeremy never took the bait. I started to realize I had found a really good thing in him. It was really like a fairy tale...until it wasn't."

Joanie didn't know Jeremy had a drinking problem at first; after all, they had met in New Orleans, during Mardi Gras, so his behavior seemed normal in comparison. Even later when certain habits began to disturb her, she would brush it off. But his prob-lem became very noticeable when Jeremy began to drink and get upset with people—mostly strangers. He had a temper that began to be revealed. Her heart sank. She tried desperately to rational-ize the behavior of the man for whom she had uprooted her life. Joanie didn't put two and two together until Jeremy started black-ing out and not remembering what he'd done.

For so long Joanie's marriage to her ex-husband had con-trolled her. After her divorce she had regained her voice and, metaphorically, found the strength to scream. Joanie wasn't going to put up with a bad relationship as she had done in the past. Not for herself and not for her kids.

It was Jeremy's drinking too much at her brother's wedding

rehearsal dinner that brought everything to a head. Joanie was stressed after having flown to Texas with the family to take care of some last-minute details for her brother and future sister-in-law's wedding. Jeremy was adding to the stress by drinking too much before and during the rehearsal dinner. He'd tried to leave the house after an argument with Joanie. When she tried to physically prevent him, he shoved her aside, and she fell and hurt her wrist. When he awoke the day of the wedding, he had no idea what he had done or what had happened but he found out from his mother. He had called her in the middle of the night, begging for help because he had hurt the person he loved.

When they returned home to California Joanie let Jeremy know that she was done. He had one more chance to get sober or she would take the boys and leave him.

It wasn't that Jeremy hadn't tried putting down the bottle. He had attempted to stop drinking many times, but every failed attempt just made Joanie angrier. She says, "To me it was a sign that he just didn't love me or our kids enough. Right or wrong, I related it to what I went through during my pregnancies. Whenever I got pregnant I stopped doing anything I thought could cause harm to my children. If I could give up alcohol during my pregnancies, I thought Jeremy should have had the willpower to do it, too, for the sake of the family."

But desperate as he was to hold on to his family Jeremy just couldn't seem to get sober on his own. Every attempt would end in a panic, a depression, a relapse more painful and crushing than the last. His fear of losing them made him reach out to his mom, Sonja, for help. Sonja's research led her to BioCorRx Recovery. It was clearly the answer she'd been looking for in order to save her son. The company produced an implantable craving-blocking drug that was accompanied by a six-month to one-year program involving coaching and counseling. The program also dealt with the emotional and spiritual side of addiction. The only problem was that it cost upward of $10,000. Jeremy had no insurance. He knew in his heart this is what was needed, but it was way too expensive to be an option.

Sonja would have gone on looking for other solutions were it not for things suddenly coming to a head. In desperation, she wrote an email to Alan Thicke, Kirk Cameron, and me. It read:

> Below are the names of the CEO and President of the program (BioCorRx Recovery) I am desperately trying to get Jeremy into. Unfortunately, I was not able to "beg, borrow, or steal" the $6–$10 thousand I need, so I am resorting to another type of begging. I would be grateful if you 3... would call and try to contact the big wigs. Jeremy is more than willing to do any type of commercials, publicity...etc., in exchange for their services.
>
> After a few weeks of trying as hard as he can to remain sober, today Jeremy took refuge in a bottle of Jack Daniels... hard liquor makes him mean...he went off in a rage, drove off drunk in his car...came home, screaming and threatening Joanie...terrifying his kids to the point of one of the kids calling the police. The police came and went in with guns drawn! Jeremy was bleeding from smashing pictures and mirrors etc... Joanie did not press charges (he did not hit her), so the cops made him leave the house because he was in a rage. Unfortunately, my Joshua has custody of Jeremy tonight. Jeremy called me, and I did not give him any comfort. Now, he's mad at me. He continues to call and text Joanie with horrible things.

*This cannot wait until it is convenient…this cannot
wait until summer…Jeremy is in a very dangerous place.
Alan, I told him about the job…he is very happy to hear
that…however, afraid it will not come true.*

*I could go on forever. My husband is in England; I fell
the day he left and tore the meniscus in my right knee. I am
no help to anyone. PLEASE…you are all smart, amazing
people…who I know love my son. I need some help desperately. Can you call the big guys and sell Jeremy's services
to them…in exchange for their program? Jeremy is willing
and ready (when he is sober). I love you all; please save
my son.*

—*Sonny*

It was this letter that drew me into Jeremy's intervention.
BioCorRx Recovery was obviously the answer Jeremy needed.
But at first, I was reluctant to help. I didn't know much about the
program, and the treatment approach was not FDA approved. It
didn't make me entirely comfortable from a medical perspective.
I also didn't have the resources of Alan or Kirk; I figured a call
from one of them would carry more weight. I was surprised that
Sonja believed I had the ability to help.

But I *wanted* to help. During my time as a medical student in
New Orleans before I was fully trained, my role had been more
about being an advocate for my patients than actually providing
care. I called BioCorRx Recovery and asked to speak to the medical director about a potential patient. I vouched for Jeremy just
as Sonja had asked, and I tried to convince the director to help
Jeremy in exchange for Jeremy's support and promotion of the
program. I was confident that Kirk and Alan would do their part
to help, too.

The year 1989 was when I first met Jeremy. In all the time since, I could never have imagined I would have had a hand in helping him overcome the one thing that threatened his happiness and, more importantly, his life. Sonja's cry for help had given me the opportunity to do for Jeremy what he had done for me— give him hope for a future. After calls from Kirk, Alan, and me, BioCorRx Recovery agreed to accept Jeremy to their program at a reduced rate.

The next steps would be Jeremy's. He began his treatment. It was a two-part process. The first step was to have an implant inserted into the fatty portion of his abdomen. Once there, it slowly released medication that would calm his cravings over the course of six months before dissolving away. The second step in the treatment plan for Jeremy was counseling to help him figure out why he drank in the first place.

Jeremy valued his relationships. Joanie, the kids, his mom, and brothers were all high on his list. I was there, too. Our relationship grew as his implant dissolved. Joanie still tells people I went above and beyond for the man she deeply loves; I want Joanie to know that it is because I love Jeremy, too. God began the process of bringing us together a long time ago through all those *Growing Pains* episodes I watched as a child.

Growing up with my heart wasn't easy. I tried so hard to feel like every other normal kid living in Jena. In many ways meeting Jeremy gave me hope of a fun, normal, successful life. It's rare for a wisher to maintain a relationship with his or her celebrity wish. It's rarer still for the opportunity to turn around and help the celebrity who once helped them. I got lucky enough to do both.

Right after Jeremy had the procedure to insert the implant in his body, they stopped at a gas station on the way home. Joanie gave Jeremy twenty to pay for the gas inside, and then she freaked.

What had she just done? She'd sent him into a store stocked with liquor, cash in hand. But she was shocked when he returned without anything to drink.

Jeremy was shocked, too. The implant was already working; he hadn't felt the need to buy any alcohol. For the first time in years, he simply walked by it. At that moment, Joanie's faith in her relationship with Jeremy was restored, and even more in God.

Jeremy has been sober since June 4, 2011, notwithstanding two short relapses. Since then he has given back. Jeremy became a spokesperson for the program. He recorded testimonial ads that aired on radio stations throughout Southern California and eventually worked directly with patients as a patient advocate. He has helped people who suffered from alcoholism in much the same way that I was caring for patients with congenital heart defects.

Jeremy and I never discuss how much we've done for one another. As Jeremy says, the feeling is mutual and true love doesn't keep score. It just pals around with hope and faith, looking for the next opportunity to give of itself. For two guys living totally separate lives I was able to help Jeremy soar in the same way he helped me reach new heights when I was still so very young and searching for hope. We've taken our lives, broken in parts, and built a complete circle.

CHAPTER TWENTY-SEVEN

A THUNDERBOLT MOMENT

After leaving Mayo Clinic I began working for a practice in Texas where I became a part of a team of five pediatric cardiologists. It was my first real job after fellowship, and I was proud to begin working for a man who had built his practice from scratch. He had a good reputation and was well-respected in his local community. I knew I could learn a lot in my new position. And for a time, I honestly felt I was exactly where I was meant to be.

Unfortunately, before I began, the practice was sold to a major corporation. Things changed. There was new leadership and the schedule became uncomfortable and rushed. Throughout my medical training my empathy for patients and my ability to connect with them and their families had been my strength. The practice just wasn't a good fit. I was considering a different position that had already been offered to me and was more in alignment with my philosophy of work: *A physician's bedside manner is just as important as how smart he or she is.* Those were the words Dr. Vargo had instilled in me as a young child when I was his patient so many years ago, and I never wanted to let go of that wisdom. I called the children's hospital in Corpus Christi, and I had a position in its cardiology department in less than a week.

At Driscoll Children's Hospital, I was charged with taking care of the outreach clinics and working with the resident physicians. My time was spent traveling by plane to McAllen, Eagle Pass, and Laredo, towns down near the border where I cared for patients who could not travel to Corpus Christi for evaluation. I also traveled to the outreach clinic in Victoria, Texas, located between Houston and Corpus Christi, as often as twice by car and once by airplane each week. Doctors in these towns referred their patients to my clinic if there are cardiac concerns.

I liked the work I did in South Texas. Other physicians in the hospital often commented about the intensity of my travel schedule, but I enjoyed it. I really felt that I was making a difference. Plus it was such a pleasure to work with my staff. With all of the travel I had the opportunity to truly get to know them, and we laughed together every day. When work is fun it doesn't really seem like work at all.

In September 2016, I accepted a position with Ochsner Hospital for Children in West Monroe, Louisiana. I would be closer to my family and would get to work with Dr. Terry King, a legend in the field of pediatric cardiology. His pioneering work in heart catheterization procedures helped advance the field of interventional cardiology, thus paving the way for further advances and helping many patients get the treatment they needed without open-heart surgery.

A month after moving to Louisiana I flew to Houston to catch up with Kirk Cameron at one of his Love Worth Fighting For events. The conferences, which are held in churches in different cities throughout the country, are designed to strengthen and encourage marriages. Even though I am a single guy I have had the opportunity to attend a few of them over the years. They are very inspiring and a lot of fun. Kirk makes jokes and interacts with the audience throughout. I got to hang out with Kirk before the show, then help his son Jack sell books and merchandise, hang out with staff backstage, or watch from the audience. When I told a member of Kirk's event staff that I had recently started living and working in West Monroe, I was informed that an upcoming conference was scheduled to be in Haughton, Louisiana, in April 2017. Since West Monroe is just some eighty miles away from Haughton, I was asked if I could help find a church that could host an event in West Monroe the same weekend.

Kirk's movie *Revive Us* was in theaters soon after my trip to Houston. I asked Dr. King and his wife, Nancy, to see the movie with me, and we all loved it. A few days later, I asked Dr. King if he knew of any churches in the area that were large enough to consider hosting one of Kirk's marriage events. He immediately called his pastor from my office and we hosted the conference at his church.

The chance to spend time with Kirk and Jeremy doesn't come around that often, so whenever it does I really try to bask in the moment. Jeremy and Joanie Miller made a special trip in to join Mama, Brenda, and me at Kirk's West Monroe marriage conference.

Besides having my family there, it was amazing to see so many people from my hometown of Jena at the event! I got to introduce a few of my childhood friends to Jeremy and Kirk. The other amazing thing is that it was Jeremy's first time at this particular event. He had heard Kirk speak before, but not like this. He was getting to experience it with Joanie by his side.

Kirk, recognizing the significance, graciously acknowledged Jeremy's presence in the audience, even asking him to join him on stage twice.

Around 4:00 a.m., I was awakened by a tremendous clap of thunder. I moved to the window and saw black clouds rolling across the sky. As I made my way back to my bed in the dark, rain began to fall, dropping slowly at first and then rising into a cacophony of noise. There was no going back to sleep at this point. All I could do was lie there pondering the events of the day. It was then that I realized that something really special had happened.

It wasn't a coincidence that we were all in West Monroe together to see Kirk. The plans for it had been set in motion years before, even though none of us were aware of it at the time. I couldn't help but think that in some way the wish I had made over two decades ago, and all the events it had set into play that had culminated in my helping plan the event, might play a role in preventing another child from going through the pain I had felt from my parents' divorce. The words Kirk spoke were meant to strengthen relationships; perhaps they would even help those I knew and loved, Jeremy and Joanie included.

A few hours before we went to the event, I sat on the couch with Jeremy and Joanie discussing our plans for the rest of the weekend. Jeremy told Joanie, "Doc is in New Orleans at Jazz Fest!" He explained to me: "'Doc' is Dr. George Fallieras, the medical director for BioCorRx Recovery."

Dr. Fallieras had not yet started working for BioCorRx Recovery when I called to see if they would help Jeremy, but I knew I had heard the name George Fallieras before. I asked to see a picture, but before Jeremy could even produce one on his cell phone, I'd pulled out my yearbook from medical school. There he was! Dr. Fallieras was one of the residents I worked with on a pediatric internship in my final year of school. We had worked a few overnight calls together. I remember him well because I still owe him money for the dinner he'd bought during one of our call nights together. I had planned to buy him dinner on our next call, the last one. But then my father passed away and I missed it. I had worked with Dr. Fallieras just two weeks before reconnecting with Jeremy.

He had always had a soft spot for people struggling with addiction. For him, it has been hard to see so many of them misjudged and disregarded. After doing his due diligence, reading and researching about the program, he joined BioCorRx Recovery Program in 2013 and has helped hundreds of people since. Though the procedure has no patent yet, they are seeking FDA approval for the medication. Jeremy and Dr. Fallieras had appeared on *Dr. Oz* together in 2016 to discuss the success of the treatment.

I shook my head and laughed, amazed. These coincidences, weaving throughout my life and the lives of those I love, show me how connected Jeremy and I really are and how destined we were meant to play a major role in each other's lives.

Dr. Fallieras says he remembers hearing about me from Jeremy, but he never connected the dots. He actually realized I was the friend Jeremy must be staying with in Louisiana while he was at New Orleans Jazz Fest; you see, I wasn't the only one looking at pictures that weekend and feeling the pieces fall into place. Dr. Fallieras knew me before he knew Jeremy, but we would both have a profound effect on him and would both end up calling him our brother. When we finally reconnected afterward Dr. Fallieras said it makes sense where I finally ended up.

A year after the *Growing Pains* cast came to New Orleans

while I was a resident at Texas Children's Hospital, some of the Tulane residents were displaced to Houston after Hurricane Katrina devastated New Orleans. The night before Katrina, Dr. Fallieras was working in the ICU at the New Orleans VA hospital. When the Code Gray evacuation alarm sounded he was one of the last to leave the hospital. After things settled he worked in Houston for four months before getting back to New Orleans. We never crossed paths in person while he was in Houston. I only knew he was there because I saw a picture of him with some of the staff. But we had not seen or heard from each other since 2004 until Jeremy mentioned his name in my living room in West Monroe.

The connection between the three of us is quite unique. First Jeremy and I met through a wish on the set of *Growing Pains*, then Dr. Fallieras and I met because of a wish fulfilled through medical school. Finally, Dr. Fallieras and Jeremy met because of a wish made to BioCorRx Recovery by Sonja and advocated by me. We all met for a reason. We all set aside our pride and made our wishes, and we were repaid a thousandfold. This is what happens when you wish upon a star and fate plays its part!

CHAPTER TWENTY-EIGHT

COMPLETING THE CIRCLE

I'm grateful to have lived beyond twenty years of age. Things are stable with my health but I am committed to yearly evaluations to make sure it stays that way.

I sometimes tell my patients about my medical condition. But sometimes the nurses and office staff beat me to it. Not many physicians become pediatric cardiologists. When I passed my boards in 2012, I was issued certificate number 2,600 since the American Board of Pediatrics started offering the exam in the 1960s. Being a pediatric cardiologist with a repaired congenital heart defect is rare enough but the fact that my teammate in Corpus Christi, nurse Chris Donald, had one as well is simply amazing. We are a testament to the fact that adults with congenital heart disease are surviving and thriving. I hope we are an inspiration for the young people who have similar concerns about their own mortality and quality of life.

I met Chris when she was a nurse in the neonatal ICU. One day while on hospital rounds she told me about her heart condition. Meeting another adult with congenital heart disease is always like meeting a member of your family. I was the first adult Chris had met who was living with congenital heart disease. Our bond was solidified when I discovered that she had been treated at Mayo Clinic by Dr. Francisco Puga, who had also performed my heart surgery there. Ultimately not only did I become her cardiologist, but she accepted a nursing position in the cardiology clinic. Since Chris had worked with all of the physicians in the practice it meant a lot that she chose me to be her physician. And we make a great team. I was sad to leave her when I moved to West Monroe—but soon afterward, her husband landed a faculty position at the University of Louisiana in Monroe. When I initially asked about Chris working in our clinic I was told that we didn't have an open nursing position available for her. A few weeks later one became available and Chris and I are working together again! In another amazing coincidence, she and her husband found a house on my street; our homes are just two stop signs apart. Not only are Chris and I back together as a physician-nurse team, but now she's my neighbor, too!

Having a heart defect in common with my patients allows me to bond with them in a very unique way. Some of them come from broken homes. As in my home, the stress of having a sick child can destroy families. My hope is to get my patients' parents to realize they need to work together. I would sometimes rather forget my childhood experiences, but God does not let me. He knows I need to use them to help others.

I work a clinic or two a month at St. Frances Cabrini Hospital in Alexandria, Louisiana—the hospital where I was born. Growing up Mama used to take me all the way to Houston for care. I always thought I would end up practicing at Texas Children's Hospital, but I don't think that was ever God's plan for my life. I am happiest just caring for patients. It is all I've ever wanted to do. Where I've ended up just feels like home.

In addition to patient care, I enjoy teaching students and residents. For the past three years, my Tulane mentor Dr. LeDoux has invited me to be a guest lecturer for the school's second-year class. I cover novel and emerging areas in pediatric and adult congenital cardiology. There are now more adults than children living with congenital heart defects, I explain, thanks to amazing advances in medicine. As patients like myself age, we need doctors with a special skill set—not just an understanding of hearts that have acquired disease with age, but an understanding of the anatomy of hearts with congenital defects, the surgeries we've been through, and the diseases we are susceptible to as adults. A new generation of patients living longer than ever before requires a new generation of doctors.

The first year I lectured someone asked why I went into pediatric cardiology. "I didn't choose it, it chose me," I said. There was a gasp in the room when I explained my answer. I love sharing my passion for pediatric cardiology with the next generation of doctors.

***

I still think about statistics and mathematics a lot because that's how my mind works. I'm still the same kid who used to program his computer alone in his bedroom. And I know the odds of all these seemingly "random events" coming together to make up my current life are truly astronomical.

The field of pediatric cardiology can sometimes feel small when it comes to the vast universe of medicine. I could say that it was a coincidence to eventually work with many of the doctors who treated me when I was a baby and an adolescent, but again, it was more than that. When someone defines something as a coincidence, they recognize that its occurrence is derived from a series of actions that have a relationship to one another. And that this relationship, for the most part, is based on fate or, for those of us who believe, God.

From the time I was born the coincidences began. Dr. Vargo, who cared for me as a child, would go on to be my advisor and the inspiration for my life's work. Jeremy, whom I admired, would become involved in my life in ways I could never imagine. These and a number of other events in my life directly aligned with one another. I'll admit I didn't see many of them until after my Starlight Children's Foundation wish was fulfilled.

Today, when I look out the window in my West Monroe office, I see the building that houses what was once my local ABC affiliate. I used to tune into that station to watch *Growing Pains* every week. My mind flashes back to 1989, when I walked onto the set of the sitcom to meet Jeremy Miller and he asked me where I went to church. We were kids—strangers, really—but Jeremy wanted to know something deeper about me, right off the bat. He wanted to know where I placed my faith. Of course, the One I placed my faith in had been instrumental in bringing us together.

Like Jeremy, Kirk also talked to me about faith. He told me that God had a plan for my life. In doing so, with very few words and not much fanfare, he confirmed the prayers Mama had spoken over me my entire life and caused me to recall all of my own quiet conversations with God.

I didn't give up on the notion that I would one day see Jeremy again, even though time, distance, and ever-changing circumstances stood between us. I settled on praying for him while encouraged by the series of events that pushed me toward my dream of becoming a doctor…and eventually, back into a relationship with Jeremy. The timing of our meetings, the people we knew being connected by various threads, and the memories of our time together drove me toward what would become my destiny and led me back around to the people I love.

***

Many of my thoughts for this book began to take shape when I was honored by my hometown of Jena, Louisiana, on May 2, 2014. The town declared that day to be "Dr. Brandon Lane Phillips Day," and the mayor presented me with a key to the city. It was a time of reflection. It was a joy to see people from my town whom I had known since my childhood. The bank teller who used to give me suckers in the drive-through window was there, as was the pediatrician who first diagnosed me with a heart murmur. Many of those in attendance had given my family money to help cover the cost of taking me to Houston for surgery as a young child. It was humbling, to say the least.

Jeremy came to Jena for the presentation, asking if he could say a few words in support of me. Before that day Jeremy had never really traced back our relationship. But now, having to stand before my family and friends, he took stock of the role we had played in each other's life. He spoke before me that day, tears in his eyes, expressing how clear it was to him that God had a part in our relationship.

I want you to know that Jeremy helped me when I needed it. And I had the added blessing of being able to help him when he needed it most, too.

Kirk was right all those years ago. God has a plan and a

purpose for my life. Yes, I have imperfections. Like many heart patients I think of a day when I will have to undergo another procedure. Maybe more than one. I know the clock is ticking and often wonder when my next procedure will be. My heart is never really "fixed." I used to wonder whether when the time came for my next procedure I would just choose to live out the remainder of my life without going under the knife again. I had outlived my expectation of making it to my twentieth birthday and had seen many items on my bucket list come to fruition.

I came to realize that my determination to live and succeed defines me more than my heart defect does. So when I listened to my own chest with a stethoscope and heard my pulmonary valve leaking earlier this year, I knew what I had to do.

On December 13, 2017—just a week ago, as I finished the process of writing this book—Dr. Cabalka performed my heart catheterization. She replaced my pulmonary valve by going through the vein in my leg, helping me avoid another open-heart surgery. This technology had first been implemented successfully at Mayo Clinic while I was there as a fellow. When I returned to my room following my procedure, I asked my nurse to borrow her stethoscope. The murmur I heard earlier this year was gone. On the day of my procedure, many of my former colleagues and staff I had worked with at Mayo Clinic stopped by to say hello; I was struck by a sense of being surrounded by family again here. By the next morning my heart's function had improved, and I was discharged after only one night. Brenda and I visited Dr. Cabalka's home the morning after my release and marveled at her beautiful Christmas tree—just as we had done during my fellowship.

I had traveled to Los Angeles just before the operation to visit Jeremy, Kirk, and other friends. While there, Kirk's boys told me that their dad was soon bringing them on their annual duck-hunting trip to West Monroe, Louisiana. The trip had been tentatively scheduled for early December before my trip to Mayo Clinic, but due to the fires in L.A., it had been delayed. Kirk wasn't sure when they would get to come.

I texted Kirk while I was at Mayo Clinic to let him know my procedure had been a success. Kirk told me he was bringing the boys to West Monroe on Sunday, which happened to be the same day I was flying home after my procedure. Kirk and his boys were arriving in the afternoon; Mama, Brenda, and I were scheduled on the evening flight. Imagine our surprise when I boarded the flight and saw that not only had Kirk and his boys ended up on my flight due to a delay but they were also randomly assigned the seats directly in front of me. A little message from God, telling me everything would be all right.

I think back to my childhood. I had planned my life on a twenty-year scale, but I have more energy at forty than I did in my early twenties. Yes, I know my new procedure will only start the clock over and begin the waiting for the next procedure. But I have a lot of living to do in the meantime and a lot of patients to care for. I carry both my physical and emotional scars into my practice of medicine, but I can't imagine life being any other way. Tomorrow is not promised but it is an exciting time to be alive and to encourage others through their journey. And regardless of the flaws in my heart, I made the decision all those years ago to open it up to hope. I made the decision to open up to my instincts, to trust in God, and to open up to love—and that love saved me.

I know God's got me—just as He's got Jeremy, Brenda, Mama, and all the people I care about. What are the odds of my receiving all that I have? Who would I be were it not for my family, friends, colleagues, and patients? I'm a pediatric cardiologist now. But deep down I'm still that little boy with the heart defect who made a wish. I wished for a family like I saw on *Growing Pains* and I've ultimately come to have a sense of family with both Kirk and Jeremy. God brought people into my life for different purposes— my TV family, the nurses and doctors I've worked with and who have cared for me, and the other patients I've met—and once our paths have crossed they've become like family. They aren't blood related, but they are family just the same.

When I was a child, some people felt that my dreams were too big. But with God, my reality is better than I could ever have imagined.

PHOTO SECTION

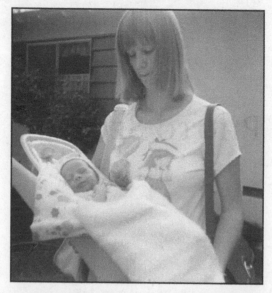

Jeremy and his mom when he first came home from the hospital

Gram rocking Jeremy to sleep

Jeremy's first day of school

Jeremy and his brother Josh at Disneyland

257

Josh, Jeremy, and their mom getting into the Christmas spirit

Jeremy's first photo shoot with his *Growing Pains* castmates,
Alan Thicke, Joanna Kerns, Tracey Gold, and Kirk Cameron

Jeremy and castmates, Tracey Gold and Ashley Johnson,
saying goodbye after 7 years of laughter and love

Cast photo for the first *Growing Pains* reunion movie. Kirk Cameron,
Tracey Gold, Alan Thicke, Ashley Johnson, Joanna Kerns, and Jeremy Miller

Jeremy with his mother while attending culinary school

Jeremy and his brother Josh during Jeremy's struggle with alcoholism

Joanie brings her boys to meet Jeremy's family. Nigel, Sonny (mom),
Joanie, Jeremy, Shaye, Vance, Sean, Josh (brother),
Tanner (brother), and Adam (brother)

Jeremy cooking in China

One of Brandon's early trips out to California after reconnecting with his *Growing Pains* family during the filming of the second reunion movie in New Orleans. Carolyn and Brandon Phillips, Nancy and Ashley Johnson, Jeremy Miller, Nigel Southworth, Barbara and Robert Cameron

Jeremy and Joanie at the premiere of the documentary *CinemAbility*

Jeremy's boys

Shaye, Joanie, and Jeremy celebrating with Sean and Cheyenne
on their wedding day

An early picture of Brandon with his maternal grandparents,
George Dean and Myrtle Wagoner

We look way too serious to be on vacation.
Brenda, Brandon, Carolyn, and Jerry Phillips

Brandon getting ready for Christmas

Wish Day on the set of *Growing Pains* with actor Kirk Cameron

Celebrating Daddy's Retirement

At the beginning of medical school

Reunited with actors Kirk Cameron and Jeremy Miller on the
New Orleans set of the second *Growing Pains* reunion movie

Taken during my residency at Texas Children's Hospital with my heart surgeon
(Dr. Denton Cooley) and my pediatric cardiologist (Dr. Tom Vargo)

Celebrating being named Louisiana Tech's Young Alumnus of the
Year with family and friends

A little unplanned surprise on my flight home from Minnesota
after getting a new heart valve

SAMARITAN'S PURSE®
Children's Heart Project

Samaritan's Purse is a nonprofit Christian relief and evangelism organization led by Franklin Graham that works worldwide in the name of
Jesus to help victims of disaster, disease, poverty, famine, and war. The
Children's Heart Project is a ministry of Samaritan's Purse that provides
life-saving operations for children born with heart defects in countries
where surgery is not available. www.samaritanspurse.org

Starlight Children's Foundation creates moments of joy and comfort for
hospitalized kids and their families. For 35 years, Starlight's programs
have positively impacted more than 60 million critically, chronically, and
terminally ill or injured children in the U.S., Canada, Australia, and the
U.K. With your help, more kids and their families will enjoy Starlight
Gowns, Starlight Fun Centers, and other Starlight programs at a children's hospital or healthcare facility near you. Support Starlight's work by
visiting www.starlight.org